sabrina's dirty deeds

sabrina's dirty deeds

month
by month
garden
chores
made easy

Sabrina Hahn

FREMANTLE PRESS

First published 2016 by
FREMANTLE PRESS

Fremantle Press Inc. trading as Fremantle Press
25 Quarry Street, Fremantle WA 6160
(PO Box 158, North Fremantle WA 6159)
www.fremantlepress.com.au

Reprinted 2017, 2020.

Consultant editor: Naama Amram
Cover and illustrations: traceygibbs.com
Index: Shelley Campbell
Printed by McPherson's Printing, Victoria, Australia

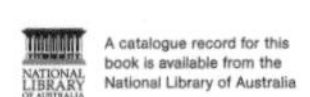

ISBN 9781925162714 (paperback)
ISBN 9781925162738 (ebook)

Fremantle Press is supported by the State Government through the Department of Local Government, Sport and Cultural Industries.

Contents

Introduction **8**

January **11**

- Creating a bushfire-safe garden 11
- Waterlilies in the garden 14
- Pest watch 16
- All regions 17
- Tropical/Subtropical 18
- Temperate/Mediterranean 21
- Cool/Cold 23

February **25**

- Making compost 25
- Going bananas 27
- Pest watch 29
- All regions 29
- Tropical/Subtropical 34
- Temperate/Mediterranean 36
- Cool/Cold 38

March **40**

- The humble sweet pea 40
- Growing asparagus 42
- Pest watch 44
- All regions 44
- Tropical/Subtropical 47
- Temperate/Mediterranean 49
- Cool/Cold 51

April **54**

- Crop rotation 54
- Spring-flowering bulbs 58
- Pest watch 63
- All regions 64
- Tropical/Subtropical 67
- Temperate/Mediterranean 70
- Cool/Cold 72

May 75
Grow your own spuds 75
Growing garlic 78
Pest watch 81
All regions 82
Tropical/Subtropical 86
Temperate/Mediterranean 88
Cool/Cold 91
June 94
Brassicas 94
Pollination 96
Pest watch 100
All regions 101
Tropical/Subtropical 103
Temperate/Mediterranean 105
Cool/Cold 108
July 111
Rose pruning 111
Partnering up for fruiting success 117
Pest watch 120
All regions 120
Tropical/Subtropical 123
Temperate/Mediterranean 126
Cool/Cold 128
August 131
Blueberries 131
A dog-friendly garden 134
Pest watch 136
All regions 138
Tropical/Subtropical 141
Temperate/Mediterranean 143
Cool/Cold 145
September 148
The benefits of predatory insects 148
Lawns 149
Pest watch 154

All regions 154
Tropical/Subtropical 157
Temperate/Mediterranean 160
Cool/Cold 162
October **165**
Tomatoes 165
Strawberries 166
Pest watch 171
Fruit fly 172
All regions 177
Tropical/Subtropical 180
Temperate/Mediterranean 182
Cool/Cold 184
November **188**
Summer-proofing your garden 188
Peanuts 190
Pest watch 192
All regions 192
Tropical/Subtropical 196
Temperate/Mediterranean 198
Cool/Cold 201
December **204**
An aesthetically pleasing vegie patch 204
Growing cucurbits 207
Pest watch 214
All regions 214
Tropical/Subtropical 217
Temperate/Mediterranean 220
Cool/Cold 222
Acknowledgements **225**
About Sabrina **226**
A–Z index **228**

Introduction

If you are quite new to gardening it can be a bit daunting – there is so much information out there it's hard to know where to start. This book will certainly help you skip along the green pathway to make our planet more sustainable, give the basics required to grow your own and hopefully get you hooked on gardening.

In writing this book I have moved from the traditional times of the seasons because climate creep has made a big difference to when we do things in the garden. We have to acknowledge that climate change is affecting plant growth and we either embrace it and change our gardening practices or experience failure.

Climate is a very tricky business in Australia. We have about thirty different zones, which I have reduced to Tropical/Subtropical, Temperate/Mediterranean and Cool/Cold or I would still be writing when I'm a hundred years old. Australia is a huge landmass and timing for planting, sowing and pruning will be different for each zone. The table opposite will help you determine what climate zone you fit into. What you need to know is the number of days above 15 degrees in your area – these are your growing days. Temperatures below that will slow down the growth rates of all vegies and fruiting plants.

It's tough stuff for those who live in the inland northern parts of Australia because they experience half of the year above 36 degrees, yet plants also have to adapt to minus temperatures at night during the dry season. In this

SIMPLIFIED CLIMATE ZONES
BY GROWING DAYS

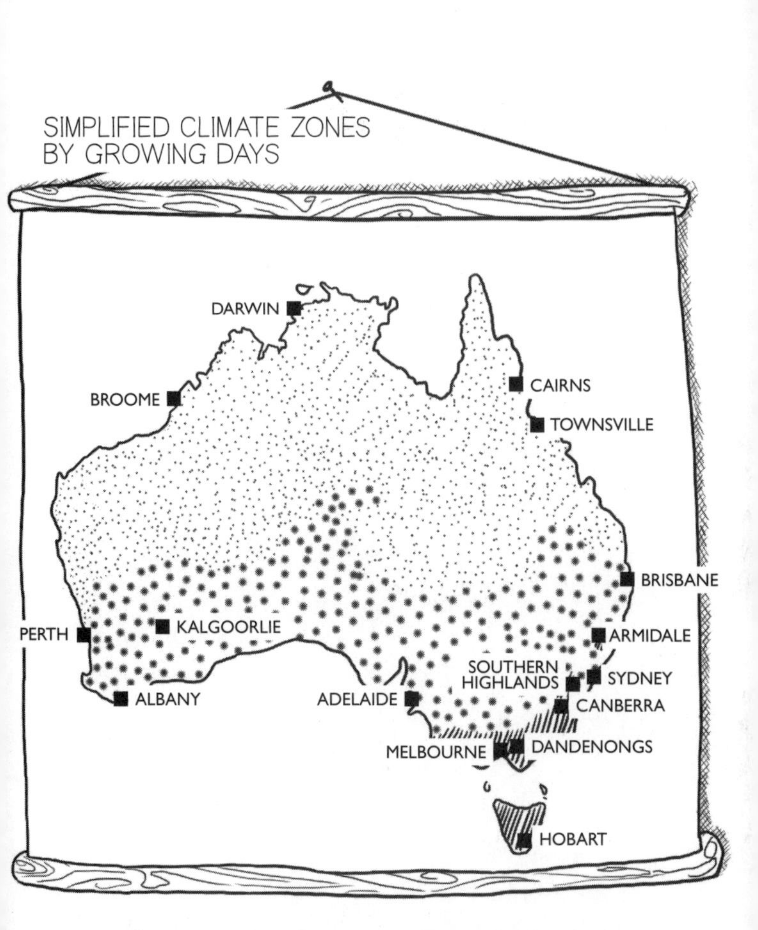

	Climate type	Growing days	Examples
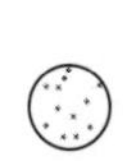	Tropical/ Subtropical	over 250	Darwin, Brisbane, Perth (coast), Broome, Cairns, Townsville
	Temperate/ Mediterranean	150–250	Perth (hills), Melbourne, Sydney, Adelaide, Kalgoorlie
	Cool/Cold	up to 150	Canberra, Hobart, Dandenongs, Armidale, Southern Highlands (NSW)

situation, it is best to plan your garden to cope with the heat, not the cold.

I have lived and worked in many different parts of Australia, from Cairns to Melbourne, the Snowy Mountains to tropical Kimberley, the arid inland of the Pilbara and the green mild climate of northern New South Wales. I understand the enormous differences in gardening due to the variability of soil types, individual seasonal weather patterns and spikes of extreme heat and cold – factors that determine what we grow and how and when we grow it.

I have been a long-time organic gardener and in this book you will find softer solutions to pest and disease control rather than broad-spectrum insecticides that affect others in the food chain. There will be at least one predator for every pest, so if you use pesticides every time you see a pest in the garden, you will be wiping out the good guys with the bad.

The same can be said for fungicides – there are so many beneficial fungi and bacteria that are essential for soil and plant health, so if we use fungicides indiscriminately it will be detrimental to those organisms whose job it is to keep the balance.

Finally, don't forget gardening is about connecting with the natural world. So don't be afraid to get your hands dirty and just have a go.

January

Creating a bushfire-safe garden

This is the time of year when anyone on a property takes a long hard look at how fire-safe their house and gardens are. There is a lot of good quality information available that offers practical advice on making your home less susceptible to bushfire attack.

One of the most important aspects of fire-proofing your home is developing a fire-resistant garden. This takes into account the overall garden design, plant species, spacing and selection of trees, hard landscaping materials, and amount of maintenance required to keep it safe.

Many people live in the hills or buy bush blocks because they love living in the bush and being surrounded by nature. It is a beautiful sight to be overlooking majestic gum trees but if they are within 20 metres of your house, they will pose an enormous threat if a bushfire is approaching.

The best trees to plant around the house in bushfire-prone areas are either deciduous trees or evergreens that have waxy leaves – like citrus, arbutus, cape lilac, harpephyllum and stenocarpus. The spacings between trees are vitally important; you don't want to form a ladder for fire to jump from tree to tree. There should be maximum separation between tree canopies and vegetation that grows on the ground beneath them (see more on p. 13).

When selecting plants for areas close to the house, think about them in terms of flammability. All succulents are a perfect choice. Waxy-leaved plants like lilly pilly, coprosma, kalanchoe and aeonium are fire-resistant, as are saltbush, some eremophila, and silver-foliaged plants like lamb's ear, santolina, snow-in-summer and olearia. Plants with a milky sap like frangipani and euphorbia are good choices too, remembering that most plants with a milky sap are poisonous. It's a bit of yin and yang.

If you have the water, plant lawn around the house – it's one of the best ways to slow down low-burning fires. If you do the right soil preparation and grow a broad-leafed, drought-tolerant lawn such as Sir Walter Buffalo or Palmetto, it will not only prevent the fire from crawling up to your house but also have a wonderful cooling effect for the whole home.

Do not mulch your garden beds with woodchips or peat-based mulch – that will feed the fire and allow it to creep underneath the mulch, progressing through the garden. Use stone or gravel around the house garden, build stonewalls if possible or place large boulders to create gaps in the garden.

If the worst happens and a fire goes through your property, there are a few basics that will help you regenerate your garden:

- Do not prune anything. If there is the slightest sap flow, your plants may reshoot once they get water. Wait until cooler months before pruning back to where the new shoots are emerging.

- Do not fertilise any plant. They are already under severe stress and there will be no vegetative growth to take up nutrients.
- Cover the ground with whatever you can get hold of. Soil erosion is the number one threat: if all vegetation has been burnt to the ground, the soil will be open to wind and water erosion. The heat will have destroyed the biological life in the soil and it will take time to recover the fungi and bacteria growth to sustain plant life.
- Apply a wetting agent so any water actually penetrates further into the soil profile.

Top Tips for a Fire-Resistant Garden

- Create a defendable space between the fire front and your house by planting out a low-flammable garden with stone or gravel paths.
- Plant deciduous trees around the house rather than eucalypts, and space them so that canopies don't meet.
- Prune lower branches of trees up to 2 metres from ground level, and rake up any bark or dead leaves under shrubs.
- Use stone or gravel as a mulch around the house. Never use woodchips or peat-based mulch.
- Use succulents, lawn and other fire-resistant plants around the house. Check the flammability of all species.
- Never place plants close to windows where they will come into contact with the glass.

Waterlilies in the garden

A garden pond with bright blooming waterlilies makes for a beautiful sight and gives the impression of tropical luxuriance.

There are two main types of waterlilies – hardy and tropical.

The hardy waterlilies are so named because they tolerate low temperatures. They come into flower in November–December and flower through to April. The colour range of the hardies is yellow, pink, white, cream, crimson and red. You need to leave the hardy waterlilies undisturbed for some years, but you can sever off the divisions and pot them up into separate containers.

Tropical waterlilies need to grow in warm water for the best flowering. They start to flower in the hot weather around January and continue through to May. Tropical waterlily flowers are on long stalks that raise themselves above the water. They come in a beautiful range of blue, white, cream, yellow, mauve and apricot. Their stamens are stunning as they are tipped the same colour as the petals.

For the home gardener who grows waterlilies in their own pond, you will need to pot up your waterlilies in either a mesh cage or a large pot that will last for at least two years. I personally don't like to use mesh cages as this leads to nutrient loss that fouls the water. You are better to pot them into a large pot with an aquatic planting mix with added cow manure and blood and bone. Add some crushed stones to the top of the pot to prevent flow-off of soil.

All waterlilies are heavy feeders and need lots of fertiliser. You can buy slow-release waterlily fertiliser tablets that can be pushed down into the bottom of the pot. You will need two tablets per pot at the start of spring and again in summer.

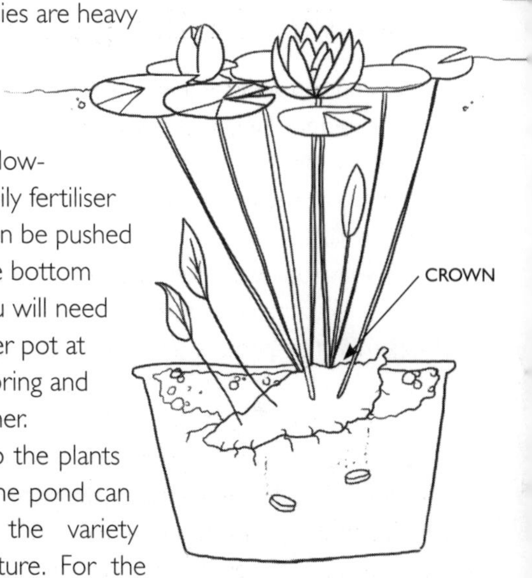

CROWN

How deep the plants are set into the pond can depend on the variety and temperature. For the tropicals, plant in shallower water until they reach a good size. Mature tropicals can have the crown 40–50 cm below the surface of the water. For the hardies, go up to 50–60 cm. Once your waterlilies are full and robust they can go as deep as one metre from the crown.

If you want your waterlilies to produce lots of flowers you will need to make sure they have at least six hours of sunlight a day. Some growers suggest that if the plant is near a pump or source of moving water, they do not produce flowers. I have not found this to be the case with my waterlilies, particularly the hardy waterlily that sits right next to the pump and flowers profusely. Perhaps cascading water tumbling onto the crown of the plant may inhibit flowering, but a more gentle movement does not seem to adversely affect them.

Waterlilies are relatively free of any major pests and diseases. From time to time aphids might attack the leaves but if you hose them off into the pond the fish will knock them off. It's a great idea to stock your pond with native fish as they will act as pest controllers. Dragonfly nymphs also help by eating mosquito larvae. Dragonflies and ponds go hand in hand, so with the added colour of waterlilies, you are in for a feast of tropical splendour.

Pest watch

January is a busy time for pests because there is a lot of new growth on plants. Most insects like to eat plants that have juicy leaves. This time of year you'll be inundated with all the sap-suckers, chewers and piercers, including aphids, citrus gall wasp, citrus leaf miner, fruit fly (see pp. 172–7), leaf-eating ladybird, pear and cherry slug, scale, two-spotted mite, whitefly and webbing caterpillar.

Two-spotted mites can be controlled with powdered sulphur or with predatory mites. A winter spray with Eco-Oil or similar organic botanical oil will help control overwintering eggs.

The webbing caterpillar will attack many native plants – you will see the tell-tale signs of frass or sawdust emerging from a hole that the borer has made to tunnel into the branch. You can either get a paperclip and skewer the grub if it's still there, or just prune off the affected branch and destroy it.

Pear and cherry slugs attack a variety of fruit trees (they are the larvae of a sawfly). Spray the tree with

Success or Dipel, or dust with diatomaceous earth, wood ash or talcum powder.

Do not use pest oil when temperatures are above 34 degrees.

All regions

- Top up mulch. Mulch can break down over time and will need to be kept at 5 cm deep to be effective. In bushfire-prone areas use stone or gravel – never use woodchips or peat-based mulch.
- Apply a wetting agent. This can be either liquid or granular, but whatever you use, it must be activated and pushed into the soil. After application turn the nozzle of the hose to jet stream and water, water, water. This will take some time, but it's worth it.
- Check reticulation – sprinklers can break and sprayers can get blocked with calcium, sand or ants. You should be checking the water is going where it's needed once a fortnight. Use the most water-efficient sprayers – don't have a fine mist being blown everywhere except the garden. The best time to water is in the morning as the moisture will dry up by the evening, making it less inviting for fungal spores to settle. Most plants prefer a deep watering and this will encourage the root system to go further down into the soil.

- Keep all water features clean from algae. The hot weather and sunshine will increase the water temperature, making ideal growing conditions for algae. Try to cover 50 per cent of the pond with plant material to cut down the amount of surface area exposed to sunlight and scoop off any slime growth weekly.
- Take tip cuttings from rosemary, lavender, azalea, geranium, pelargonium, succulents, camellia, duranta and gardenia and pot them up in cocopeat to propagate.

Handy Hint

Refill birdbaths with fresh clean water every day in summer. You will be rewarded by the best workers in the garden coming to stay.

Tropical/Subtropical

Edible garden tasks

- Sow artichoke, basil, beans, broccoli, cabbage, Cape gooseberry, capsicum, chilli, Chinese cabbage, chives, cress, cucumber, eggplant, galangal, ginger, kohlrabi, leek, lemongrass, melon, peanuts, pumpkin, radish, rosella, silverbeet, spring onion, sweet corn, taro, tomato, watermelon, zucchini.
- Plant out banana suckers into improved soil (see pp. 27–9). They are best grown in afternoon shade

to help conserve moisture. Grow them in clumps of at least three and flood plants every three days. Bananas are heavy feeders so use a good quality fertiliser with all the minerals and high potassium. Prop up large bunches of bananas with a forked stick if the weight of them is pulling over the stem. Once the stem has fruited, cut it off at the base because it will never bear fruit again.

- Prune all the lower branches of avocado, mango, citrus and figs to prevent the spread of fungal diseases that are transmitted to fruit from rain splash. You can foliar-spray fruit trees with copper hydroxide to prevent foliar fungal diseases.
- Net all summer fruiting trees against fruit bats and birds. It seems that they love to dine on the same fruits we do. Somehow it puts me off sinking my teeth into a mango that a fruit bat has chowed down on. I'm not sure of their dental hygiene. Use white wildlife-friendly netting that bats and birds won't get tangled in.

General garden tasks

- Apply a 30 per cent shadecloth over the vegie garden to keep moisture in the plants and the extreme midday heat off the leaf tissue. Make sure there is plenty of ventilation.
- Ensure your compost is not getting too wet during the summer season – always have a bale of dry hay or straw to help keep up the carbon content (see p. 25).

- This is the weedy season in the tropics and weeds will take over your garden if allowed. Get on top of them before they seed to save yourself a lot of work later in the season.
- Fertilise the whole garden now, particularly fruit and vegies, as the rains will leach out nutrients. Plants are growing rapidly at this time of the year and they will need the aid of a good quality fertiliser with all the minerals for healthy growth.
- Powdery mildew may attack roses, dahlia, crepe myrtle, pumpkin, cucumber, watermelon and begonia – apply either EcoCarb or a solution of 50/50 full-cream milk and water.
- Prune back any brittle branches from trees in preparation for summer storms.
- Prune back bougainvilleas to keep them in check. If you are training them up a trellis or fence line, it's the best time to prune while it's hot.
- Tip-prune poinsettias and abutilons to stop them from getting leggy.
- Lift and divide these tropicals to make more plants: caladium, ginger, hippeastrum and eucharis lily.
- Propagate azaleas by laying a piece of stem along the ground and anchoring it with a piece of wire or brick. In 4 weeks time it will have formed roots – sever it from the parent plant and put it into a pot.

Temperate/Mediterranean

Edible garden tasks

- Sow Asian greens, beans, beetroot, broccoli, cabbage, capsicum, carrot, celery, Chinese cabbage, chives, cress, cucumber, eggplant, kohlrabi, leek, melon, mustard, radish, rosella, silverbeet, spring onion, sweet corn, taro, tomato, zucchini.
- Summer-prune early stone fruit, apples and pears to keep the trees at a manageable size and keep the energy going into fruit production.
- Prune back table grapes by thinning out bunches and allowing better air circulation. The quality of bunches will be much better and grape size larger.
- Keep an eye out for the two-spotted mite and spray with Natrasoap.
- Apply grease bands around pear and apple trees to capture female codling moths.
- Mulch around berry plants (raspberry, boysenberry etc) with a mixture of straw and manure and water deeply.
- Apply a 30 per cent shadecloth over the vegie garden to keep moisture in the plants and the extreme midday heat off the leaf tissue. Make sure there is plenty of ventilation.
- Do not let parsley and basil form seed heads; harvest them regularly. Once the seed stem has formed the leaves will become bitter.

- Cut off runners from strawberry plants (see p. 168) and pot them up into good quality potting mix.
- Hand-pollinate all your cucurbit plants such as pumpkin, watermelon, rockmelon, cucumber and zucchini early in the morning. In the peak of summer the pollen may have dried out later in the day when bees are about. Be the bee.

General garden tasks

- Keep the water up to hydrangeas, and control powdery mildew with either EcoCarb or a solution of 50/50 full-cream milk and water.
- Prune back the long twining growth of wisteria to prevent it from taking over your garden, house, shed, the neighbour's shed etc.
- Raise the blades on the lawnmower to preserve moisture in the ground and not expose leaf blades to summer heat. Leave the lawn clippings on the surface to recycle the nutrients back into the lawn.
- Lightly trim spring-flowering natives 20 cm back from spent flowers to keep them bushy and compact.
- Lightly trim back lavender and rosemary to get continued flowering and fresh growth.
- Lift and separate gerbera plants. Spacing them will allow them to form more flowers and prevent powdery mildew.

- Lift and divide bearded iris. Discard the old rhizomes as they will not flower again.
- Plant out autumn-flowering bulbs such as autumn crocus, nerine, haemanthus, belladonna lily and Josephine lily.
- Plant out Louisiana iris while playing some bluegrass music – it makes your knees feel better.

Cool/Cold

Edible garden tasks

- Sow Asian greens, basil, beans, beetroot, broccoli, brussels sprouts, cabbage, capsicum, carrot, cauliflower, chives, cress, kale, kohlrabi, leek, lettuce, onion, parsnip, radish, rhubarb, shallot, silverbeet, spring onion, swede, tomato, turnip, zucchini.
- Potatoes can be planted out now while the soil is still warm. Use seed potatoes and always practise crop rotation – never plant potatoes in the same soil two years running.
- Mulch up around sweet corn and tomato plants – their aerial roots will take up nutrients and help produce better cobs and fruit.
- Harvest zucchini and cucumbers every day as they grow rapidly and will be woody when too old.
- Prune raspberry, currant and gooseberry vines wearing heavy-duty long-sleeved gloves and long trousers.

- Peaches, nectarines and Japanese plums can have a light prune immediately after flowering to produce the growth for the next season's fruit.
- Look out for brown rot forming on stone fruit. (A winter spray of Kocide or copper oxychloride will prevent this problem from occurring in summer – see p. 128, bottom.)

General garden tasks

- Lay snail pellets or traps around hostas and dahlia plants coming into flower. I think hostas must be an aphrodisiac for snails – they attract every gastropod for kilometres.
- Apply sulphate of potash to all plants in the garden – it keeps them healthy during this rapid growing period and protects them from disease.
- Repot tuberous begonias into cocopeat or a potting mix and apply a slow-release fertiliser.
- Divide and replant cymbidiums.
- Lift and divide bearded iris. Discard the old rhizomes as they will not flower again. Out with the mother, in with the daughter.

February

Making compost

There is nothing more satisfying than making compost. Good compost is like gold and gardeners crow like a rooster when it comes out black, crumbly and smelling sweet.

There are countless books on making compost and it can look very complicated, but basically it's all about the amount of carbon (dry/brown) bits and nitrogen (wet/green) bits that go into the heap. The smaller the bits, the faster it breaks down.

The vital ingredients for compost are:

- Carbon
- Nitrogen
- Oxygen
- Water

Carbon (dry/brown) matter includes straw, hay, autumn leaves, sugarcane mulch, wet cardboard, shredded newspaper and woodchips.

Nitrogen (wet/green) matter includes fresh lawn clippings, animal manures, blood and bone, garden prunings, green leaves, kitchen food scraps, tea bags, coffee grounds and eggshells.

If your heap is made up of 60 per cent dry matter and 40 per cent wet matter, your compost should work.

The most efficient size for a compost heap is one cubic metre.

Cover your heap – it keeps the heat in and hopefully the vermin out. You can use old carpet or a tarp – something that's easy to move every time you want to add to the heap.

Make the bottom layer about 10 cm of hay and then the next layer kitchen scraps, lawn clippings and manure. Keep alternating the layers and remember to water after every dry layer. Some gardeners like to mix half a cup of molasses to 9 litres of water when they moisten the heap.

The heap will start to heat up. Leave it for 5 days before turning it over to distribute the bacteria throughout the pile. You can turn the heap every two weeks.

A good way of getting air into the centre of the heap is to push a length of polypipe with holes drilled through its sides into the centre. Oxygen will get into the hottest part and feed the bacteria.

There isn't a single plant that won't benefit from compost added to the soil. Compost feeds other soil microbes, buffers against high or low pH, retains moisture in the soil and helps plants to resist the bad soil-borne fungi and bacteria.

You can spread compost on top of garden beds and cover it with mulch; you can dig it into the top 5 cm of soil and you can definitely use it in the planting hole. Once you've made your first beautiful batch of compost, you will be hooked.

Handy Hint

I always have a bale of lucerne hay at the ready to mix in with the food scraps.

Going bananas

Bananas are such a great plant, even without the fruit. The plants are ornamental and edible and the leaves are sensational to wrap food in. If you live up north, you can plant them at this time of the year, taking advantage of the rains in the wet season.

You can either buy a plant from the nursery or dig up a friend's sucker from their banana clump. Choose a sucker with sword-shaped leaves rather than one with rounded leaves, as the latter takes much longer to fruit. Always try to get some of the root, and let the suckers dry out for a couple of days before planting out. This will help prevent root rot.

Bananas are very heavy feeders so you will need lots of compost, poo and a good quality fertiliser in the bottom of the hole. Bananas love old chicken manure. Add a good handful of dolomite lime and sulphate of potash after planting.

If possible, grow a few banana plants in a pit. Dig it 60 cm deep and fill it with all the good stuff. Because they like a fair bit of water, use water storage crystals in the bottom of the hole. They fruit much better if you flood them every three days. To do this, build a moat around the banana tree so the water collects around the base and sits there draining slowly into the ground without escaping.

Each banana is called a finger, and the fingers form a hand. The hanging cluster of hands is called a bunch. Once the bunch has formed it will take about two months to ripen. When the flower at the bottom of the bunch begins to dry out and go brown, and the bananas are almost full-sized, cut the flower off. The flower is delicious when cooked in a stir-fry or a curry. Cover the bunch with a plastic bag that is tied at the top but open at the bottom. This will protect the bananas and help the ripening process. However, it will not stop rats from gathering their banana entrée.

When the fingers are full and the colour is just changing from green to yellow, chop the whole bunch off and hang it in a cool shady spot. Always pick from the top down, only one hand at a time. To ripen more quickly, store the hand with a ripe banana or apple.

The parent plant will only fruit once because it is actually a herb (I know, a pretty big one), so cut it down at the end of summer and allow two suckers to grow in its place.

Pest watch

Do not use pest oil when temperatures are above 34 degrees.

Keep beer traps full. Check every evening as snails are on patrol.

Keep fruit fly baits fresh. Always pick up fallen fruit from the ground, put it in a sealed bag and cook it in the sun or put in the freezer before binning it (see pp. 172–7).

Hibiscus beetle may be chewing the leaves of shrubs – you can spray with Eco-Neem or pyrethrum.

If you see small pimples on leaves, you have lilly pilly psyllids on your plant. They will be harbouring underneath the pimple indented into the underside of the leaf. Simply tap the leaves to get the psyllids to drop onto the ground, where they struggle to survive.

All regions

February is a busy time for plants, pests and gardeners, so don't forget to rest, hydrate and stay inside during the hottest time of day – early morning or late afternoon is a perfect time to get your hands dirty in the garden.

General care

- This is the fastest time to make compost – there's plenty of green waste and heat. Have some lime and blood and bone handy to throw on each layer. Remember to turn regularly to distribute the bacteria that breaks everything down. Keep the heap in a shady spot and water if it gets dry.
- Protect newly planted seedlings from the heat with plastic pots, cardboard or shadecloth.
- Apply a liquid fertiliser to autumn-flowering bulbs and always water in well.
- Feed liliums as they die down, to give the bulb energy for next season's flowers.
- Give cymbidiums in pots a really good soak every evening and add a few ice blocks to the top of the pot – the flowers will be much better.
- Apply Epsom salts at the rate of 1 teaspoon to 5 litres of water to the foliage and root zone of citrus, gardenia, palms, murraya and abutilon.
- Liquid-fertilise house plants and check for pests such as scale. If house plants are leggy and pale, move them into more light. Never put them outside if temperatures are above 34 degrees – they will go into shock, go brown, have dead bits and hate you so much they will fall into a deep depression and die.
- Make sure the worm farm is getting enough moisture – it can dry out very quickly in February. Keep the cover moist by spraying with water in the morning.

The edible garden

- Apply a liquid fertiliser to all vegies, particularly greens like lettuce – they need to grow fast.
- Feed rhubarb plants weekly with a liquid seaweed solution and liquid fertiliser. Keep mulch away from the crown.
- Sweet corn needs to be hilled up with hay and watered heavily as the cobs form.
- Harvest eggplants when they are young – they are susceptible to sunburn this time of the year and are much sweeter when young.
- Choose an area to plant out sweet peas in March–April (see pp. 40–2). Add 1 handful of dolomite lime to the area with some compost and dig in well.

Natives

- Prune back summer-flowering natives. All can be safely pruned back by a third, which keeps them more compact and disease-free.
- Fertilise all native plants with a slow-release fertiliser that is designed for natives – these have low phosphorus levels and trace minerals.

Lawn

- Sow lawn seed or lay roll-on turf, it will establish very quickly at this time of the year. Do some homework to see which is the best lawn variety for your soil type and climate. Steer clear of cheap couch lawn as it's a terrible invasive weed that gets into all garden beds and bushland. It will be the bane of your life.

- Some lawns are susceptible to fungal diseases. If you see signs of a fungal disease, spray with Mancozeb Plus in the evening and do not water the lawn for 4 days. Do not fertilise for 2 weeks as the nitrogen will encourage the fungal growth.

Pruning

- Do not prune any fruit trees or heat-sensitive plants during the summer months.
- Prune any diseased plants. Don't put affected leaves or flowers in the compost bin or leave them on the ground to reinfect the other plants.
- Tip-prune all hedges to encourage autumn growth. Do not prune back hard – no more than a third.
- Thin out grapevines that have finished fruiting – it will allow more airflow and help prevent disease.
- Prune all flowering annuals that have had a few months of constant flowering. Water well and liquid fertilise – you may get another few months of flowering on the new growth.
- Prune back buddleias hard when flowering has finished. And I mean hard – I once had a limb off a lemon-scented gum fall on my *Buddleia crispa*,

flattening it to the ground. I followed through with pruning it to the ground and it's the best it's ever looked.

- Prune off agapanthus heads that have finished flowering. Take the stem off at ground level.
- Trim back geranium, pelargonium, daisy, lavender, grevillea, scaevola and hakea to keep them compact and free-flowering.
- Prune back dianella and lomandra plants – they may have become leggy and brown. You can prune them down to ground level. New growth will emerge in autumn.

Planting and cuttings

- Sow seeds of autumn-flowering annuals like calendula, marigold, nasturtium, primula, wallflower, foxglove and pansy.
- Sow fresh cycad seeds into seed-raising mix and protect from heavy rainfall.
- Nerine bulbs can be planted out now.
- Take cuttings from daphne, abelia, azalea, choisya, buddleia, hebe, gardenia, viburnum and brugmansia.
- Harvest the seed from summer-flowering annuals that have finished flowering and store them in a glass jar. You can throw them around the garden the next spring and see what pops up.
- Divide bromeliads – simply break the pups off and pot up into a 50/50 cocopeat and potting mix blend. Place pots in a shady, protected area.

- Divide up palms like golden cane and rhapis by separating the suckers from the parent plant and potting up into new potting mix. Keep them well watered until new roots develop. Do not fertilise until you see new growth.
- Divide clivia, crinum and hippeastrum bulbs.

Tropical/Subtropical

Edible garden tasks

- Sow Asian greens, basil, cabbage, Cape gooseberry, capsicum, Ceylon spinach, chilli, Chinese cabbage, chives, cress, cucumber, eggplant, galangal, ginger, lemongrass, melon, okra, radish, rosella, silverbeet, sweet corn, sweet potato, taro, tomato, watermelon, zucchini.
- Mango trees can be fertilised now around the drip line of the tree. Apply a fertiliser designed for fruiting trees so they get all the nutrients and minerals they need to produce fruit.
- Make sure the entire surface root system of citrus trees are getting enough water. Keep the mulch away from the trunk. Apply a liquid wetting agent to all the foliage and root system.
- Protect citrus trees from codling moth caterpillars. Pheromone traps will attract and kill the winged males; grease bands around the trunk will capture the females. In summer you can also spray with Dipel or Success every 10 days.

- Dragon fruit is just as tasty for birds and bats as it is for us – protect them by individually bagging each fruit. Liquid-fertilise weekly.
- Bananas will be growing rapidly. Make sure you have no more than three stems: one that is fruiting, one that is half the size, and a baby sucker emerging from the base of the plant. Feed them up with a well-balanced fertiliser for fruiting plants. Spray with liquid potassium or 2 tablespoons of sulphate of potash dissolved in a 9 litre watering can. (See more on pp. 27–9.)
- Harvest fresh green drumstick tree pods and slice up to put in curries and stir-fries. The tree will continue to flower and fruit. The leaves can also be eaten, cooked as you would baby spinach or in salads.
- Arrowroot and cocoyam will be found in the fruit and vegie shops or markets now – you can grow these in your own garden.

General garden tasks

- At this time of the year you cannot use any pest oil sprays, copper or sulphur sprays because they will burn your plants. The best method of control is prevention and using your fingers on insects.
- Add lime to your compost and turn regularly every two weeks. If it is out in the open, protect it from getting too wet with the summer rains.

- Get rid of summer weeds before they seed through the garden. They can be hot-composted.
- Spray natives, citrus and gardenias with iron chelates to prevent yellowing of leaves.
- Plant out summer-flowering bulbs like the pineapple lily, alstroemeria, crinum and hippeastrum.
- Ixora plants will be in full flower and attracting the beautiful blue-coloured Ulysses butterfly. Take tip cuttings now and grow a hedge.
- Take cuttings from impatiens, tuberous begonias and African violets. Plant them into a propagation mix of cocopeat and vermiculite.
- Apply a granular fertiliser to frangipani plants to prolong flowering for another few months.
- Keep gutters clean from leaf litter. There will be wet season rains and blocked gutters lead to house leaks.
- Make sure the chook house has plenty of fresh hay on the ground to keep the pen hygienic for your girls.

Temperate/Mediterranean

Edible garden tasks

- Sow beans, beetroot, cabbage, carrot, celery, Chinese cabbage, chives, cress, cucumber, eggplant, leek, melon, mustard, peas, potato, pumpkin, radish, rosella, silverbeet, spring onion, zucchini.
- Plant potatoes out now for a late autumn harvest.

- Remove the runners from strawberry plants and pot them into fresh potting mix until they form a good root system. Cut back strawberry plants that are over two years old.
- It's time to prune apple trees – but only the new growth that has formed this year. Leave all the limbs with fruit still on them. Cut back to the first two buds that form on the main branch.
- Remove any mummified stone fruit from the trees to prevent the spread of brown rot.
- Shake stink bugs into a bucket of soapy water – they will drown.

General garden tasks

- Apply DroughtShield to plants susceptible to sunburn.
- Replant cyclamen bulbs into fresh potting mix and add a slow-release fertiliser.
- Fertilise camellias and azaleas for mass flowering in late winter and spring.
- Make sure potted plants are maintaining moisture. Check to see if ants have excavated out the soil around the root system and if the water is penetrating throughout the pot. Some plants may need to be soaked in a bucket of water with a seaweed solution for an hour to rehydrate.
- Keep over-vigorous climbers in check with a prune to hold back long tendrils. Do not fertilise as this encourages more growth.

- Prune back roses lightly at the end of the month to encourage new blooms for autumn. Fertilise after pruning, but water it in really well. Make sure the mulch is still at least 5 cm thick.
- Spray iron sulphate on moss that develops in the lawn over summer.

Cool/Cold

Edible garden tasks

- Sow Asian greens, basil, beetroot, broccoli, brussels sprouts, cabbage, carrot, chives, endive, English spinach, leek, lettuce, parsnip, radish, rhubarb, silverbeet, shallot, swede, turnip.
- Tie leaves of cauliflower plants around the developing head to prevent the curds turning brown or getting sunburnt.
- Stake tomato plants as they grow and make sure sunlight is penetrating to the inside of the plant.
- Cut back blackcurrant plants by removing the oldest stems. Prune back raspberries – all the canes that have fruited should be cut down to ground level.
- Feed all deciduous fruit trees to get healthy growth before cold nights return.
- When cherry trees have finished fruiting, cut the long wispy shoots back by 50 per cent.
- Prune European plums back to the main branches – they bear their fruit in the older wood.

General garden tasks

- Deadhead roses and fertilise.
- Spray plants that are affected by powdery mildew with EcoCarb.
- Scan through your spring-flowering bulb catalogues but wait until the weather cools down before planting out.
- Fertilise camellias and azaleas for the mass flowering in late winter and spring.
- Plant out autumn-flowering crocus bulbs.
- Deadhead petunias, pansies and salvias.
- Spray ferns with water every morning to keep up humidity levels.

March

The humble sweet pea

The old-fashioned, much-loved flowers are coming back into vogue. The princess of all flowers would have to be the sweet pea. Belonging to the same family as edible peas, the sweet pea has an interesting history. If you have travelled to Malta, Sardinia or Sicily in spring, you will have seen the original and highly perfumed purple sweet pea in full flower.

The huge number of varieties available today had their beginnings in the late seventeenth century in the hands of a Franciscan monk, Francesco Cupani, who noticed a bicoloured variety had popped up in the garden of his monastery at Palermo. He collected the seed, grew it and it came up true to form. In 1699, a few years after discovering the flower, Cupani sent seeds to a botanist in Amsterdam and, it is believed, to another botanist in England. Pretty soon there were many different sports of the original purple sweet pea.

In 1793 a renowned seedsman from Fleet Street in London listed five varieties. It took a while for the sweet pea to reach its celebrity status, but by the 1800s the world went wild to get hold of different forms – royalty, vicars, botanic gardens and the commoner.

Sweet peas have the most intoxicating perfume and gorgeous flowers. Australian gardeners would traditionally plant out their sweet peas on St Patrick's Day (17 March), but with the ongoing summers, you can still plant them out until the end of May. For those who live in high-frost areas, it's better to wait until the threat of frosts is over and have your sweet peas as spring/summer flowers.

You can get dwarf, medium and tall sweet peas to suit most spaces. The dwarf forms grow really well in pots and look great in a hanging basket. Sweet peas will need at least 6 hours of sun a day and a trellis to climb up if you plant the taller varieties.

Sweet peas need a sunny position and pre-limed soil. Sprinkle dolomite lime and compost into the hole 2 weeks before direct seeding.

When planting out the seeds, push them down to twice the depth of the seed and have the soil damp. Water when you plant the seeds, but then do not water again until they have germinated and you see the first leaves emerge, which should take 10–14 days. This is the main reason gardeners lose their peas – they overwater and the seeds rot.

If you give sweet peas too much nitrogen you will get loads of healthy growth, but few flowers. Use rock dust, sulphate of potash and a liquid fertiliser.

Flowering will commence around 12 weeks after planting. Remember, the more flowers you pick, the more flowers will form. There is nothing as beautiful as a bunch of sweet pea flowers in a vase. Kids absolutely love picking them. Sweet peas are such giving plants and worth a spot in your garden every year.

Diggers Club have some beautiful heirloom sweet peas including the Spencer Ripple Mix, a variety originating from the Earl of Spencer's garden in 1901, and Matucana, renowned for its incredible fragrance. Yates have released another couple of sweet peas known as 'Pink Diana' and 'Fairy'. 'Pink Diana' has the most wonderful, large, fragrant pink flowers. It is a tall grower (up to 2 metres in height), making it ideal to cover a fence line. 'Fairy' is perfect for pots and hanging baskets. It grows to only 30 cm and is a bicoloured, ruffled pink-and-white variety. The packet is enchanting with the little May Gibbs character wrapped in a sweet pea bonnet.

When I was a kid my mother and grandmother always left a spot in the garden to plant sweet peas. Flowers are so important in the garden – they fill the air with their scent and lift the spirits with the joy of colour.

Did You Know

In the 1700s the sweet pea was referred to as 'sweet-scented pease' and became a status symbol for the wealthy.

Growing asparagus

Asparagus is a long-term crop so you need to decide where it is going to grow for many years. My mother's asparagus patch produced enough for a family of seven for at least twenty years. With a crop that stays where it's put for that long, good soil preparation is essential.

Asparagus will grow in free-draining soil with a pH of

about 6.5. They need to grow in full sun. A month ahead of planting out asparagus crowns, prepare the soil with equal parts of manure and compost. Mix this through and then add a few handfuls of dolomite lime. Asparagus are hungry feeders, so the more organic stuff you can throw in the trench the better.

You can grow asparagus from seed or crowns.

If you grow from seed you must heat-treat the seed to assist germination. Soak the seed in warm water for at least 6 hours. Sow the seeds into potting mix and cover with vermiculite. Keep in a warm position out of direct sunlight and keep moist. Seeds can take anything from 2 to 5 weeks to germinate so don't lose hope too quickly.

Most people grow asparagus from crowns. It is a faster way of getting a crop. Most nurseries will have buckets of crowns in either sawdust or cocopeat around autumn, which is a great time to plant them out. If you live in frost-prone areas, wait until spring to plant out the crowns. In tropical parts wait until July.

Dig a trench 25 cm deep and 25 cm wide into your prepared soil. If you are planting more than one row, make the rows 40 cm apart as asparagus does not like overcrowding. Make a little mound in the bottom of the trench and spread the roots of the crown over the mound. Think of it as putting a toupee over a bald head. You then cover this with around 8 cm of soil and put a 4 cm mulch layer on top. You can use pea straw, sugar cane, lupin or lucerne. Water in very well.

Do not harvest asparagus for the first two years, just allow the ferns to grow. This will give you larger crowns and better asparagus for the many years to come. Cut back dried ferns in late autumn to 2 cm above the ground. After pruning, add a layer of manure and more mulch. Then, wait for the spears to appear in late winter.

Pest watch

Do not use pest oil when temperatures are above 34 degrees.

Soft-bodied scales such as mealy bug and cottony cushion scale can be successfully controlled by predatory wasps and voracious ladybird larvae. If you spray with a pest oil or neem oil you are likely to kill these predators along with the pest. Instead, use a magnifying glass to see if predators have been at work. If there are wasps, you will see mummified bloated bodies. Juvenile ladybirds will eat the scale alive.

Caterpillars will be getting stuck into your vegies, particularly leafy greens, cabbages and kale. Spray with Dipel or Success, which is derived from natural bacteria and doesn't harm the birds that eat the caterpillars.

All regions

General care

- Transplant shrubs that need to be shifted into another position if they are failing to thrive. Always prepare the new hole and prune foliage back by a third before you dig up the shrub. Make sure the root ball is wet enough to hold the soil around the root system.

- Give all ferns a half-strength dose of liquid fertiliser.
- Cast a critical eye over the entire garden. Anything that has really struggled over the summer months and looks scrappy you may wish to move or remove. Visit nurseries and find plants that are better suited to your climate zone and soil type.

The edible garden

- Fertilise all citrus trees, particularly those that have finished flowering and started to form fruit. Ensure they are getting enough water to prevent premature fruit fall. Keep the mulch away from the trunk.
- Plant out your fruit trees while the soil is still warm: avocado, citrus, loquat, fig, mango and sapodilla.
- Give strawberry plants a liquid feed and apply a dressing of compost.
- When you have finished harvesting bean plants, leave the roots in the ground as they will continue to release nitrogen.

Lawn

- Fertilise lawns before the cooler weather arrives. Many lawn varieties are bred for warm or hot climates and their growth slows down significantly over autumn and winter.

Pruning

- Hedges of lilly pilly, murraya, box, westringia and photinia will benefit from a trim before the weather cools down.

Planting and cuttings

- Sow spring-flowering annuals either directly into the garden or sow in trays of seed raising mix. Always prepare the ground for direct seeding 10 days before sowing. Rake in some compost, wetting agent and aged sheep manure. Lightly rake the area before you sow and cover with a light mix of vermiculite and cocopeat. Always water using a mist rather than the full spray or you will wash the seeds out of the ground.
- Divide clumps of dianella, lomandra, pennisetum and themeda to replant in other areas or give to friends. Overcrowded clumps may need to be separated with a sharp spade or hatchet. Make sure you have at least 5–7 shoots on the new clumps.
- It's time to get cuttings from abelia, gardenia, daphne, buddleia, choisya, curry bush, lavender, geranium, pelargonium, teucrium, dianthus, salvia, plectranthus, viburnum and daisy.

Tropical/Subtropical

Edible garden tasks

- Sow Asian greens, basil, beetroot, broad beans, broccoli, cabbage, cassava, cauliflower, celery, Chinese cabbage, chives, cress, endive, English spinach, Florence fennel, kale, leek, lettuce, onion, peas, potato, rocket, silverbeet, spring onion, swede, sweet corn, tomato, turnip.
- Get the vegie patch ready for the autumn and winter crops. Empty out beds, apply layers of compost, manure and rock dust. You can even throw your weeds on if they are not in flower or seed. Weeds have many nutrients in their leaves.
- Plant corn where beans have grown to make the best use of the nitrogen-fixing nodules left in the ground. Always plant corn in blocks because they are wind-pollinated. Hill up compost and straw around the base of the plants once the aerial roots emerge. Corn is a hungry feeder so fertilise fortnightly with a fertiliser that has all the minerals in it.
- Fertilise banana, avocado, pawpaw and mango trees with rock dust and mulch with chicken manure and hay.
- Give fruit trees a foliar feed with liquid potash to improve the quality of fruit and keep them resistant against anthracnose.

- Harvest the mature drumstick pods and remove the peas. You can cook them up like garden peas or put them in soups. They have a delicate flavour and are highly nutritious.

General garden tasks

- Fertilise the garden after the wet season – much of the nutrient content will have leached out. All garden beds, vegetables, fruit trees and lawn will need a boost as they will have put on a lot of growth.
- Take cuttings from myrtle, cinnamon, midgen berry and dragon fruit.
- Prune back dracaenas and cordylines. Use the cuttings to make more plants.
- Tip-prune bougainvilleas to hold them back from taking over the garden and your neighbour's garden.
- Fertilise tropical plants like ginger, galangal, turmeric, heliconia and caladium as they start to go into dormancy for the dry season. If you have large clumps it's a great time to divide them up and make new plants.
- Frangipanis may have developed rust spots on their leaves over summer – spray with copper hydroxide making sure it gets to the backs of the leaves. Remove any fallen leaves as the spores will reinfect the tree.

- Sow fresh palm seeds into cocopeat and keep moist. Leave in the shade until they germinate and then shift into dappled light.

Temperate/Mediterranean

Edible garden tasks

- Sow beans, beetroot, broccoli, cabbage, carrot, cauliflower, celery, Chinese cabbage, chives, cress, endive, kale, leek, lettuce, mustard, peas, potato, silverbeet, spring onion.
- Beds that had cabbage, broccoli or kale plants can be replanted with carrot, Florence fennel, celery or parsley (see pp. 54–7).
- Plant flowers among the vegies to attract beneficial insects. Sow cornflower, lavender, marigold, pansy, snapdragon, stock, sunflower, verbena and viola.
- Check cherry, pear and hawthorn trees for the slimy black caterpillars called pear and cherry slugs. Spray with Success or Dipel, or dust with diatomaceous earth, wood ash or talcum powder.
- Control weeds underneath fruit trees by cutting and then smothering. Fertilise and then put a mulch over the top.
- Keep up the fruit fly control measures for late-ripening fruit – use Naturalure Fruit Fly Baits, Yates Nature's Way Fruit Fly Control, and replace traps regularly (see pp. 172–7).

General garden tasks

- Time to order your spring-flowering bulbs in preparation for planting out in May. Cold-climate bulbs like tulips, daffodils and hyacinths will need to go in the crisper of the fridge for 6 weeks before planting out.
- Cut the flowering stems of agapanthus when they have finished flowering. Apply a complete fertiliser to get energy back into the leaves.
- Remove summer-flowering annuals to make room for winter flowers.
- Fertilise camellias, rhododendrons and azaleas as they are budding up. Make sure they are getting enough water – apply a wetting agent and mulch around the base.
- Direct sow wildflower seeds such as everlastings for a mass display in spring. Prepare the ground 2 weeks before sowing with compost and cocopeat. Apply a liquid wetting agent and sow into damp ground.
- Sow sweet peas (see pp. 40–2).
- Lightly prune roses to encourage new growth for the autumn flush of flowers. Apply a wetting agent and a complete fertiliser with all the minerals as well as NPK. This is the best time of the year to see the colour of the flowers as the sun is less harsh on the petals. The perfume is also intense.

Cool/Cold

Edible garden tasks

- Sow beetroot, broad beans, broccoli, brussels sprouts, cabbage, carrot, celeriac, chives, English spinach, Florence fennel, leek, lettuce, onion, parsnip, radish, rhubarb, shallot, silverbeet, swede, turnip.
- Harvest pumpkins now, leaving at least 5 cm of stalk, and store in a cool dark place away from potatoes.
- Harvest beetroot, silverbeet and English spinach and crop-rotate by planting out anything in the brassica family – kale, cabbage, brussels sprouts.
- Freshen up beds with compost and manures before cold nights arrive and give everything a feed with liquid fertiliser while there are still warm sunny days to encourage fast growth.
- Move potted citrus into more protected areas away from frosts and cold winds; you may need to cover them up at night to protect the foliage from damage.
- Crabapples, medlars and hawthorns will start bringing in the birds.

General garden tasks

- Autumn colours will soon start showing on deciduous plants so it's a great time to visit the tree nurseries to find the perfect autumn foliage for the garden.
- Order and plant out your spring-flowering bulbs into prepared ground: ixia, crocus, freesia, bluebell, iris, snowdrop, grape hyacinth, anemone, ranunculus, allium and jonquil. Leave tulips until next month.
- Cover bulbs with aged manure after planting out – it will help develop the flowers.
- Apply a wetting agent to sun-drenched soils in preparation for autumn rains.
- Mow and fertilise lawns for the last time before the cold nights set in. If lawns are healthy before winter they will cope much better with frosts and recover quickly in spring.
- Plant flower seedlings such as hollyhock, cornflower, primula, poppy and wallflower.
- Deadhead perennials and prune back summer-flowering shrubs to encourage new flowering wood for spring.
- Give indoor plants a liquid fertiliser and trim off any damaged leaves.
- Prune back buddleias by two thirds. Tip-prune boronias, correas, hakeas, grevilleas and eriostemons.

- Repot cyclamens into fresh potting mix and apply a slow-release fertiliser.

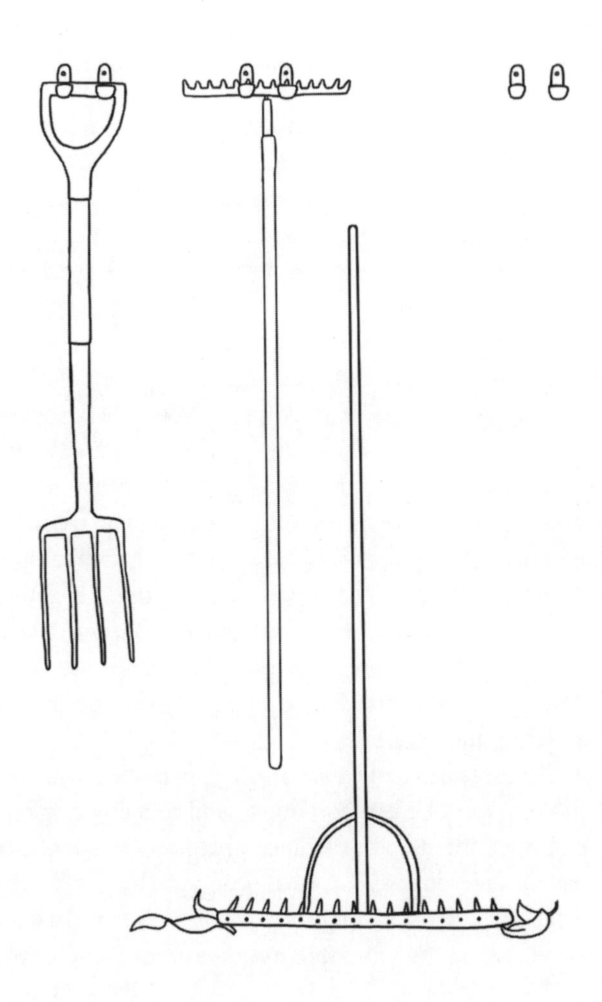

April

Crop rotation

This is the crop rotation season. The hot days are behind us and cooler weather means a change of pace in the garden and time to revamp the vegie patch.

Why bother with crop rotating? Because it is a really effective way of controlling pest and disease problems. Some vegies are susceptible to certain types of fungi or bacteria, so if you keep planting the same crop in the same position it's only a matter of time before it is attacked. All the brassica family (broccoli, cabbage, cauliflower etc) are vulnerable to club root disease and of course the cabbage white butterfly. Tomatoes are prone to getting wilt, root-knot nematode and blossom-end rot. Moving crops around and planting them among other vegies lessens the chance of a disease getting hold, breaks the cycle of pest infestation and allows certain nutrients to recycle. You will get the most out of your garden with the least amount of pests and disease attacking the vegies.

There seems to be quite a bit of confusion surrounding the rotation of crops. You don't need to study magic or pay strict attention to the lunar phases; you just need to have a few ideas about what you want to grow. Crop rotation is simply making sure that you do not plant the same crop in the same spot every year. For those of you who are thinking, 'I can't remember what I plant from one month to the next, let alone a whole year!' – that's why they invented digital cameras.

Make up a new folder in the computer titled 'How I Fed a Nation' – the date will already be on it and your vegie patch diary is created. This sort of diary is also handy to look back at what crops did well and what pests and diseases came to play with the vegies.

All the vegie plants that you have finished harvesting can now be removed from the garden beds. The soil will need to be reinvigorated with compost, manure, rock dust and worm juice. This will help feed the beneficial soil microbes. One way of getting nutrients back into the beds is to crop-rotate with a green manure crop, like broad bean, lablab, mung bean, sub clover, vetch or mustard. These plants fix nitrogen in their root system and at the end of their growing season they can be dug back into the soil.

When you decide which crops to put where, consider that each type of vegie has different nutrient and water requirements. Most vegies grow in a pH of 6.0–7.0. Peas and beans prefer dolomite lime in the soil prior to sowing. Beetroot needs boron added to get a good sized beet. Pages 56–7 show which vegies to plant together.

Remember through all this that gardening is meant to be fun. It's all about experimenting with your plot and finding out what works best for you.

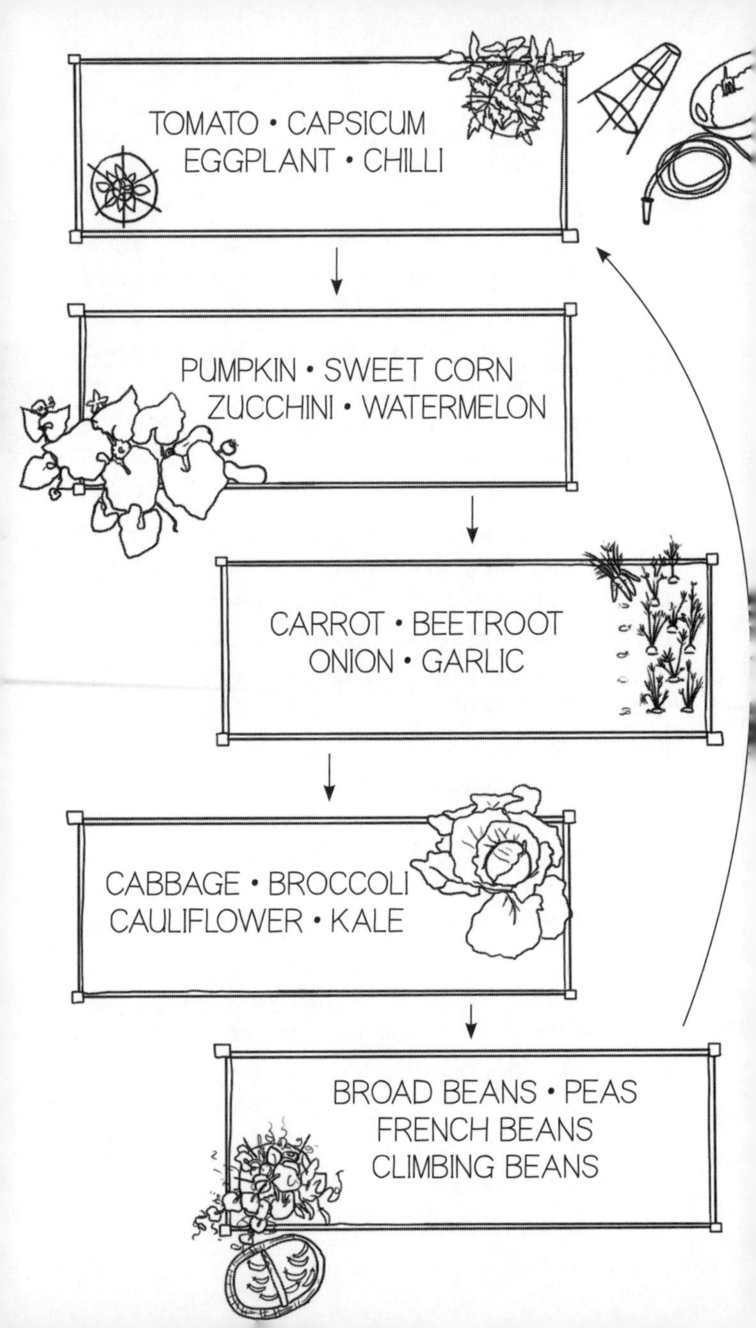
TOMATO • CAPSICUM
EGGPLANT • CHILLI
PUMPKIN • SWEET CORN
ZUCCHINI • WATERMELON
CARROT • BEETROOT
ONION • GARLIC
CABBAGE • BROCCOLI
CAULIFLOWER • KALE
BROAD BEANS • PEAS
FRENCH BEANS
CLIMBING BEANS

Family groups

Bean family (*Fabaceae*) – broad beans, bush beans, climbing beans, French beans, peas.

Beetroot family (*Chenopodiaceae*) – beetroot, English spinach, mangel-wurzel, silverbeet.

Cabbage family (*Brassicaceae*) – broccoli, brussels sprouts, cabbage, cauliflower, kale, kohlrabi, mustard, radish, turnip.

Carrot family (*Apiaceae*) – carrot, celeriac, celery, Chinese fennel, Florence fennel, parsley, parsnip.

Daisy family (*Asteraceae*) – endive, Jerusalem artichoke, lettuce, radicchio.

Gourd family, cucurbits (*Cucurbitaceae*) – cucumber, gourd, pumpkin, rockmelon, squash, watermelon, zucchini.

Onion family (*Alliaceae*) – chives, garlic, leek, onion.

Tomato family (*Solanaceae*) – capsicum, chilli, eggplant, pepino, potato, tomato.

Spring-flowering bulbs

No doubt many gardeners have been drooling over lush pictures of bulbs and wondering if they might be able to grow them in their gardens this year. The good news is yes, if you select the right bulb for your climate and do a bit of preparation. The bad news is that if you live in really hot climates you will have to treat some of them as annuals because our torturous summers make it tough to survive through to the next year. People with murderous winters have a similar problem. Some bulbs need frost over a length of time in order to flower, but nights that fall below 6 degrees when the bulbs shoot can be enough to send them to the paddock in the sky.

The bulbs you buy have all their stored food supply already to produce leaves and flowers once they are planted out. How effectively they flower and grow has been determined by their previous year's growth, so purchase your bulbs from a reputable grower. Bulbs should be fat and heavy, like they have just eaten Christmas dinner.

Most of us have the vision splendid of mass flowering, but few of us achieve it. I know I am not alone when I confess to packets of bulbs sitting in the crisper for months, until they succumb to death by chill. Either that or they sit on your verandah until guilt takes over and you plant them out three months too late.

If you are a bit of a novice and not sure how to plant bulbs out, grow them in pots where the success rate is much higher. Spring-flowering bulbs suitable for pots include daffodil, Dutch iris, jonquil, galanthus, hyacinth, leucojum, muscari and of course tulip. You can pack them in much closer than you would in the ground. You can double-stack them, with the larger bulb at the bottom of the pot and smaller ones near the top. There are specific bulb potting mixes, but any good quality potting mix with a bit of added compost will do the job. Bulbs need to grow in free-draining soils with a neutral pH. They will certainly need fertilising, but this must go down in the bottom of the pot so that the roots don't come into direct contact with it. Once the bulb shoots leaves that are around 5 cm tall, you can give them a light dressing of a general-purpose fertiliser or a liquid fertiliser. Once your bulbs flower, start to feed them up again with both a liquid feed and a slow-release fertiliser. This stage is critical to feed the bulb up for next year's flowering.

Even though you see lots of pictures with flowering bulbs indoors, they can only be brought in once they are flowering. When flowering finishes, take them outside again and allow them to die down. Three weeks after this, lift the bulbs, shake off the soil, dry them out, roll the bulbs in sulphur dust and place in paper bags in a dark cupboard. Next autumn have a go at taking the bulbs you grew in pots and planting them out in the garden.

If you want to have a crack at naturalising bulbs choose bluebells, sparaxis, freesias, jonquils, daffodils and snowdrops.

The most important thing you need to know is to plant the pointy bit up and plant them at twice the depth of the length of the bulb. There are two exceptions to this rule: ranunculus have the claws pointing down, and anemones have the pointy part downwards. Mind you, I have seen people just throw bulbs in hoping for the best, and they do seem to right themselves.

Some bulbs like their neck out of the ground or just peeping out. These include hyacinth, belladonna, hippeastrum and haemanthus. I think this is part of their character as they all develop very big blousy flowers.

A few weeks before planting out prepare the soil with cow or sheep manure and compost, then mix in a heaped tablespoon of slow-release fertiliser. This will be enough to see the bulbs through their flowering cycle. If you want the bulbs for next year you will need to fertilise again after flowering on a weekly basis until the leaves die down entirely.

If this is all too much, the nurseries have pots of bulbs in full bloom in spring and you can always tell people you grew them yourself.

Although we use 'bulbs' as a general term, some of these plants are not actually true bulbs but corms, tubers and rhizomes.

Corms

Corms are solid food storage organs formed by a thickened stem that grows underground. The main difference between bulbs and corms is that corms are solid rather than made up of layers. They can produce roots from the base as the shoots appear, or they can produce contractile roots whose purpose is to pull

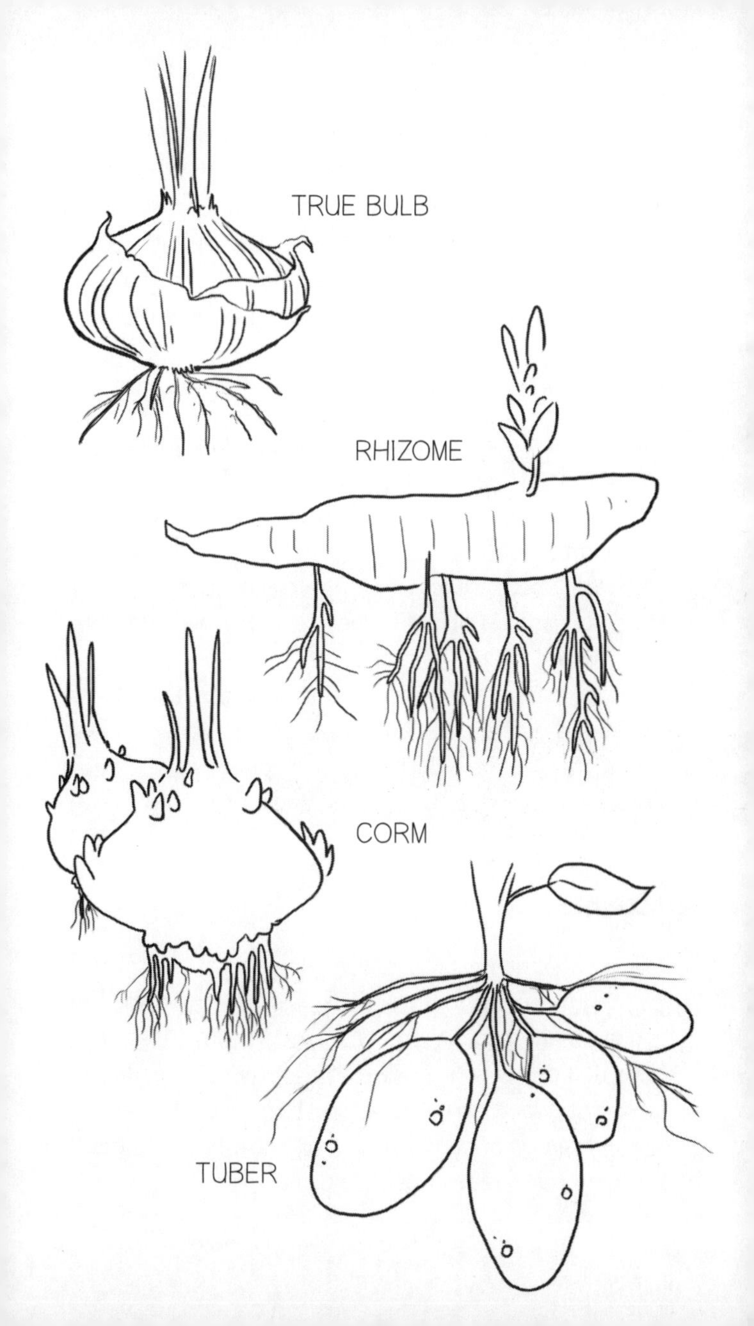
TRUE BULB
RHIZOME
CORM
TUBER

the corm deeper into the ground. Corms multiply by producing more than one new corm from the top of the old corm. When flowering finishes, the new corm that has emerged from the base of the new stem literally grows from the old corm. Examples of corms are gladiolus, water chestnut, freesia, taro, saffron and some irises.

Tubers

Tubers can be divided into two types – stem tubers and root tubers. They are simply an enlarged organ for the purpose of storing water and nutrients to survive tough conditions.

Stem tubers are formed from thickened rhizomes or stolons. Examples of stem tubers are cyclamen, tuberous begonia and of course potatoes.

Root tubers are a modified lateral root that stores water and nutrients. Examples of root tubers are sweet potato, ranunculus (which have thin spidery legs), dahlias (which have fat stumpy legs) and anemones (which have hard knobbly knees).

Rhizomes

Rhizomes are the underground horizontal stems of a plant. They spread by producing shoots at the ends of the stem and roots at the base underneath. Most of us have had plenty of exposure to rhizomes in the kitchen with ginger and turmeric. If you have ever grown and divided cannas or bamboo you will know how successful this method of growing is for a plant.

Ginger, bamboo, Venus flytrap, canna and alstroemeria are all rhizomes and can be divided up and replanted in autumn. It is essential to plant them horizontally, close to the surface of the pot or ground. Use all the same planting techniques as you would for bulbs. Liquid-fertilise until the rhizome begins to shoot, then apply a dressing of slow-release fertiliser. All plants with rhizomes benefit from being divided as the older parts become susceptible to bacterial and fungal diseases.

Pest watch

Leaf-eating ladybirds will attack potato plants, zucchini, melons, cucumbers and squash. They are larger than the common ladybird and have orange spots rather than red. They have many predators (small insectivorous birds will come and pick them off, as will assassin bugs), but if there are no predators around you can collect them and drop them into a bucket of soapy water or spray with Eco-Oil.

Whitefly can be controlled with yellow sticky traps or horticultural oil like Eco-Oil mixed with pyrethrum.

Put down beer traps for snails and slugs, or use pet-friendly pellets like Multiguard in special snail houses. Otherwise use copper tape or spray with Escar-Go.

Cabbage white butterfly will be laying eggs – spray your brassicas weekly with Dipel or Success.

Curl grubs or armyworm may be attacking lawn. You can drench with EcoGrub or lay down wet hessian or damp sheets at sunset. Early the next morning, lift back the sheets and remove the grubs by hand. If you have chickens, magpies or butcherbirds, they will do the work for you.

All regions

General care

- It's time to get inspired and redo parts of the garden – nurseries will be full of wonderful new selections of natives, ornamental shrubs and annuals.
- This is the best time to transplant just about anything apart from deciduous trees and shrubs. If anything is overcrowded, growing in the wrong place or just unhappy get stuck into it now. Always have the hole prepared and prune the top by a third before you dig the plant out. You can drench the soil and leaves with a seaweed tonic, but do not fertilise until you see new growth.
- Top up the mulch to discourage the germination of winter weed seeds. If they come through the mulch, they are much easier to pull out and you get them before they set seed again.
- Clean out your gutters in preparation for winter rains. The leaf mould makes a wonderful soil improver so don't waste it – put it on your garden.
- Adjust your reticulation system to match the cooling weather and reduced water needs.

- Cymbidium orchids should be starting to bud up now. Move them into dappled light or morning sun to encourage flowering. Keep a check on caterpillars that love the young buds.
- Apply dolomite lime to lavender hedges to keep them healthy over the winter period.
- Pinch out the tops of seedlings to encourage side shoots and better flowering. Liquid-fertilise every fortnight.
- Feed up your roses for the autumn display of flowers.

The edible garden

- Give the vegie garden a dose of worm tea – use 1 part worm juice to 10 parts water. Don't use on hakeas, grevilleas, banksias or proteas.
- Feed strawberry plants with a high potassium and phosphorus fertiliser every fortnight.
- Cut back and bundle up summer herbs to use them dried during the winter months.
- Propagate some of your favourite fruit trees by taking cuttings now. Quince, loquat and persimmon can be grown by 15 cm long cuttings that are about pencil thickness; mulberry plants can be grown from 15–40 cm cuttings. Dip them in honey, remove all the leaves and plant into a propagation mix. Fifty per cent of the cutting needs to be buried. Leave in a shady spot and water daily.

- Thin out fruit on apple, pear and plum trees to get larger and better quality fruit. This will also take the weight off the branches and prevent them from snapping off.
- Lightly prune passionfruit vines to keep them manageable and encourage lateral growth.

Natives

- This is without a doubt the best time to plant natives – trees, shrubs, grasses, ground covers and climbers. Be sure to get the native that is right for your soil type and climatic conditions; most of our native plants are very soil-specific.
- Cut kangaroo paws back to 5 cm and lift and divide clumps. It is best to plant smaller bits into a pot with potting mix so they develop roots before you plant them out.

Pruning

- Deadhead hydrangeas, but leave the big prune until July or August, after the threat of frosts.
- Keep deadheading dahlias. More flowers will come.
- Prune back plumbago plants by at least 50 per cent. Apply a wetting agent and fertiliser and water well.
- Salvias will have leggy growth – prune back by 50 per cent or wait to see where the new growth is shooting at the base of the plant and prune to just above the new shoots.

- Tree dahlias can be pruned down to ground level when they have finished flowering. Cut the stems into 30–40 cm lengths and lay them horizontally in a container and lightly cover with a propagation mix of sand and cocopeat.

Planting and cuttings

- Divide up liriope, agapanthus, shasta daisy, coreopsis, mondo grass, day lily, dianella and flax plants.
- Your favourite flowering perennials can be divided up now, including yarrow, campanula, shasta daisy, phlox, dianthus, catmint, rudbeckia, gerbera, gaura and scabiosa.

Tropical/Subtropical

Edible garden tasks

- Sow Asian greens, basil, broad beans, broccoli, cabbage, carrot, cassava, cauliflower, celery, Chinese cabbage, chives, climbing beans, cress, cucumber, daikon, eggplant, endive, English spinach, leek, lettuce, potato, rocket, silverbeet, spring onion, swede, sweet corn, sweet potato, tomato.
- Peas will almost grow before your eyes. Plant them directly into ground that has been prepared with dolomite lime, compost and aged sheep or cow manure.

- Keep planting out tomatoes – they will crop over the dry season but will require watering. Plant them deeper into the ground; they will develop roots all up the stem.
- Plant out new strawberry runners into a mix of compost, manure and potting mix. Keep them off the ground, out of the reach of lizards and snails.
- Get mulch onto all garden beds in preparation for drier weather; keep it away from the trunks of trees and shrubs.
- Keep the water up to ginger and turmeric plants. They will store it in their roots and be tastier and larger when they are harvested in June.
- Propagate yams by cutting up and dividing the tubers into 6 equal pieces. Dust them in powdered sulphur and leave them to dry in a cool, dark place for 10 days. Plant them into pots of potting mix one-third deep (that is, with two thirds of the tuber sticking above the soil). They will develop shoots 4–5 months later and can then be planted out into the garden. Yams will need a support to grow up and lots of rotted manure and compost in the soil. They will be ready to harvest about one year later.
- April is a great time to get citrus trees established – orange, lime, lemon, grapefruit and pomelo. Plant into soil that has had compost and manure added and drenched with a seaweed solution. Remember that citrus trees have a wide root run and are surface feeders, so make the hole wide and mulch after planting.

- Spray pawpaws with wettable sulphur to reduce the incidence of fungal diseases.
- Prune back mango trees that have finished fruiting. Apply a fertiliser and rock dust after pruning.
- Harvest tamarind pods. The pulp is fantastic in cooking and can be frozen for months.

General garden tasks

- Lawns may have developed moss over the wet season – you can increase the pH of the soil with lime and spray the area with iron sulphate. Always remove the moss after spraying so it doesn't come back to life.
- Keep bulbs in the crisper this month. Leave planting out until the rains have subsided.
- Get stuck into canna lilies, heliconias and ginger plants. Cut off all dead leaves and weak stems to ground level, fertilise and water well. Remember to replace the mulch around the base of the plants.
- Liquid-fertilise everything. Pour it over the leaf tissue as well as the root zone.
- Spray for black spot and other fungal diseases. Pick up any diseased leaf tissue or fruit.

Temperate/Mediterranean

Edible garden tasks

- Sow artichoke, asparagus, beetroot, broccoli, cabbage, carrot, cauliflower, celery, Chinese cabbage, chives, coriander, cress, daikon, endive, Florence fennel, garlic, kale, kohlrabi, leek, lettuce, mustard, onion, parsley, peas, potato, radish, silverbeet, spring onion, swede, turnip.
- It's time to order your bare-rooted berry bushes like raspberry, boysenberry and brambleberry. Most berries like a slightly acidic soil with lots of added compost and manure. They will need a trellis system to help keep them under control and make pruning easier. Plant them in rows and mound up the soil to a height of 15 cm. Once you have planted the canes, mulch with lupin, lucerne or pea straw.
- Spray peach and nectarine trees with Kocide or copper oxychloride as leaves drop to control peach leaf curl.
- Clean up strawberry plants by cutting them right back and planting out the runners into soil that's been topped up with manure and compost.
- Remove the heads off beetroots and carrots as soon as you harvest them as the moisture will be robbed from the root. Beetroot leaves are wonderful in a salad or stir-fry.

- Brassicas like cabbage and kale will need liquid fertilising to keep them actively growing over the cooler months.
- If you have heavy clay soils, improve the drainage before the rains appear and make the ground too soggy and wet to dig.

General garden tasks

- Mow your lawn and fertilise for the last time until spring. Make sure the moisture is reaching the root zone and keep a check on algae growth.
- Banksias and correas are looking sensational. Cut banksia flowers and bring them into the house – they last for weeks in a vase.
- Gardeners who are hoping for an early break in the rain must check to see if the water is penetrating to a deeper level in the soil. Dig down with a hand trowel and if it's dry twice the depth of the trowel, apply a wetting agent. Make sure you water it in well so that the precious rain is delivered to the subsoil.
- Thin out citrus fruit buds to get better quality and larger fruit. The tree can't support all the fruit that forms and will drop it anyway.
- Prune back callistemons and melaleucas that have finished flowering. Prune by one-third and take out any dead wood.

- Lift and divide dahlia plants. Cut stems back to 4 cm above the tubers and shake all the soil off. Dust tubers with powdered sulphur and store in an old stocking in the shed until spring.

Cool/Cold

Edible garden tasks

- Sow Asian greens, asparagus, beetroot, broad beans, broccoli, brussels sprouts, cabbage, carrot, celery, chives, coriander, daikon, dill, endive, English spinach, Florence fennel, garlic, kale, kohlrabi, leek, parsley, radish, rhubarb, shallot, silverbeet, spring onion, swede, turnip.
- Remove the old woody canes from raspberry plants and blackcurrant bushes. Leave the young green ones, which will bear next season's fruit. Tie up the new canes to the trellis.
- Protect susceptible plants like chilli, eggplant and tomato from the cold by placing a shield of bubble wrap or plastic tree bags. Make sure your shield is staked well.
- Harvest all pumpkins before the cold nights hit – they will not tolerate frosts.
- Spray peaches and nectarine trees as the leaves fall with a copper-based spray.
- Prune apricot trees before the cooler months to prevent infection from fungal diseases that may enter through pruning wounds.

- Wait until the frosts come to harvest your apples – it makes them sweeter.
- Apply one handful of dolomite lime per square metre to new plantings of vegies and to apple trees to avoid bitter pit.
- Give a dressing of sulphate of potash to broad beans.

General garden tasks

- Lift and divide lily-of-the-valley bulbs and tuberoses – they will flower for you the following year.
- Liquid-feed indoor plants and move them towards windows that get more winter light.
- Remove all the dead flowers and spindly growth on perennials and herbaceous plants.
- Shape maple and silver birch trees by thinning out branches. Do not cut their tops off as this will ruin their shape. The idea is to create an evenly branched tree through selective pruning, opening up certain areas of the tree to highlight the branches.
- This is the best month to transplant evergreen trees or shrubs. Make sure you have the hole prepared and ready before you dig up the existing tree. Apply a wetting agent and water the area thoroughly before digging around the root mass. Keep as much soil around the root system as possible.

- Lift and divide herbaceous peony roses. They may not flower for a year, but will bloom profusely the following year.
- Dahlias can be cut back and stored away for the winter. Leave 10 cm of stem, shake off some of the dirt and store them in the shed until spring.

May

Grow your own spuds

The humble potato is one of the most nutrient dense vegetables to put on your plate. They are practically fat-free and have vitamins C, B1, B3, B6, folic acid, potassium, phosphorus, magnesium, calcium, zinc and iron. The Incas obviously understood the health benefits of the spud as they cultivated it extensively from the thirteenth century onwards.

Potatoes need a sunny open position with free-draining soil and lots of goodies as they are hungry feeders. Don't let your spuds dry out, but don't overwater. They will need regular feeding with a good quality organic-based fertiliser with minerals, humic acid and fulvic acid.

Potatoes are great to grow in containers that you can add layers of hay to, or a wire cage that's packed with straw to create walls.

As with any crop, preparation is everything.

Step-by-step guide to growing potatoes

1. Prepare the area with aged pig, cow or sheep manure. Try to avoid fresh manure as this can cause rotting problems – it's best to put manure in at least three weeks before planting out the tubers. Cover this with a layer of lupin, lucerne or pea straw, then a layer of compost. Sprinkle with a general-purpose fertiliser and water in well.

2. Dig a trench along your bed 10 cm deep. Place the seed potatoes 25 cm apart, with 30 cm between rows. I have used Kipfler, Ruby Lou and Royal Blue. Fill in the trench with soil and add a 10 cm layer of lupin, lucerne or pea straw. Drench the rows with a seaweed solution and water in well.
3. Water every 3 days until green shoots appear above the straw. When these reach 15 cm high, hill them up with lupin, lucerne or pea straw so that the top 5 cm of leaf is showing. Drench with liquid fertiliser and seaweed solution.
4. As the leaves emerge from the straw a few weeks on, keep hilling up with lupin, lucerne or pea straw, add a sprinkle of blood and bone fertiliser and drench with seaweed solution. Every third straw layer, spread a few handfuls of compost.
5. About 20 weeks later, your crop will be ready to harvest. Some potatoes flower, but others may not. If you are unsure of the size of the tubers, just have a little dig and check them. If you intend to store your spuds, let the tops die off completely before harvesting. It is easy to harvest with a fork. All that beautiful mulch and compost can now be used on your green leaf crops.

Potato varieties

Carlingford

White skin and flesh. Excellent for salads, boiling and roasting, but not good for chips. Available all year.

Delaware
A good all-rounder with cream-coloured skin and white flesh. Available all year.

Desiree
Long oval shape with pink skin and yellow flesh. Excellent for boiling, roasting and salads, but not so good for frying. Available all year.

Kestrel
Has blue eyes and cream flesh. A great spud for frying and chips, and excellent in roasts, mash and salads. Available all year.

Kipfler
Elongated with yellow skin and flesh. Excellent mashed, boiled, steamed or baked. Not suitable for frying. This one is only available November–January.

Mondial
Yellow skin and flesh. Makes great mashed potato and good for salads, roasting and steaming, but not suitable for frying. This one is only available August–October.

Nadine
Cream skin and white flesh. This is a great one for salads and steaming. Does not make good chips, but excellent mashed. Available all year.

Royal Blue

The all-purpose spud with purple skin and yellow flesh. Great mashed, boiled, roasted, fried or in salads. This is one of the best potatoes for chips. Available all year.

Ruby Lou

Dark pink skin with white flesh. Another good all-rounder that makes great roast potatoes. Available all year.

Handy Hint

Never store your potatoes with onions as the onions give off a gas that makes them spoil faster. Instead, put an apple in with your potatoes – it will delay their sprouting.

Growing garlic

May is the perfect time to plant out your garlic bulbs. Freshly harvested garlic tastes divine compared to the dried-out bleached bulbs that adorn the vegie shelves of supermarkets.

Get your garlic from growers' markets or shops that sell local organic garlic. Some of the supermarket garlic has been sprayed with an inhibitor to stop them from sprouting and prolong storage – these will not sprout in the garden. Go for full bulbs that have a bit of weight in them. It's best to use fresh garlic that has not started shooting. Any papery cloves should be discarded.

Prepare the soil with good quality compost and sheep manure at least 2 weeks before planting out.

Apply a handful of gypsum and sulphate of potash to a square metre prior to planting. Garlic prefers neutral to slightly alkaline soil and will not set good bulbs if it has an excess of nitrogen.

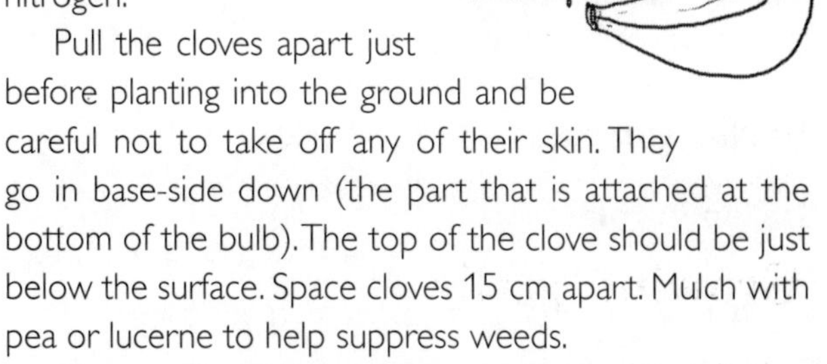

Pull the cloves apart just before planting into the ground and be careful not to take off any of their skin. They go in base-side down (the part that is attached at the bottom of the bulb). The top of the clove should be just below the surface. Space cloves 15 cm apart. Mulch with pea or lucerne to help suppress weeds.

Cloves will develop a root system first and then a week later green shoots will appear. Water in well and give the soil a drench with a seaweed-based solution. You can apply seaweed and an organic liquid fertiliser once a month, but it shouldn't need any other fertiliser after planting.

Garlic is a long-term crop, taking up to 8 months to mature, so plant it where it won't be disturbed by other crop rotation. Harvesting usually takes place in summer – late November or early December. It's important to allow the soil to dry out a few days before harvesting. The bulbs are ready to lift when the base of the neck looks papery and the tips of the foliage dry off at the top.

My grandmother used to say, 'Plant garlic on the shortest day of the year, and harvest on the longest.' I find that works most of the time, unless a garlic-loving labrador comes along and harvests it for you.

Pull the garlic up with the leaves attached. Brush off the dirt – do not hose it off. You can plait bunches together and leave hanging in a cool, dry place. Do not store garlic in the fridge as cold temperatures initiate sprouting.

Check out what varieties are available in your local area and plant out a few different types to see which variety suits your conditions best.

Garlic varieties

Italian Purple

This is one of the earliest varieties to harvest. It suits most climate zones and has beautiful purple cloves.

Italian Red

Perfect for the really cold climate zones that experience frosts. This variety is usually planted out in early March because it can tolerate frosts.

Italian White

Ideal for the Mediterranean climate gardeners. A large bulb that produces up to 20 cloves.

NZ Purple

A smaller but sweeter bulb with a really lovely nutty flavour.

Southern Glenn

If you live in the tropics this will be the best variety for you.

Pest watch

Snails will be on the move early in the morning and late in the evening. Place beer traps and little houses to hold pet-friendly snail pellets. Get the ones that have holes too small to allow lizards and possums.

Citrus leaf miner will still be around – you can spray foliage with Eco-Oil or use the eco citrus leaf miner traps (Eco-CLM trap).

Put up sticky strips to catch unwanted pests. Replace when the strips are 80 per cent covered by insects. Use a magnifying glass to make sure you are not trapping beneficial insects.

Cabbage white butterfly will be into the brassicas – you can lay exclusion netting over crops or spray regularly with Dipel or Success.

Look for scale and mealy bug harbouring on new flowering buds and down at the base of the plant. Spray with horticultural oil like Eco-Oil.

Keep an eye out for borers of eucalyptus, banksia and wattle. If you see sawdust coming out of a stem or the trunk, move it away and you will see a hole – poke a piece of wire into it and shishkebab the grub.

All regions

General care

- The garden will require much less water now, so reduce your watering. There may be early rains, the evaporation levels are much lower and there will be dew left on the ground in the mornings.
- Reduce the watering to all indoor plants now their growth rate is slowing down.
- Move all potted plants that cannot withstand the cold mornings into a more sheltered position on a north-facing wall. Cover if necessary.
- Continue to transplant any evergreen that needs shifting before the soil gets too cold to inhibit root development. Stake it until new roots develop to anchor it to the ground.
- Check out bare-rooted shrubs and trees that will become available in nurseries over the next couple of months.
- Never waste autumn leaves – they are a valuable resource to add to the garden. You can either put them straight into garden beds or add them to the compost heap. A little scattering of blood and bone will help them break down quickly.
- Remove rootstock from any plant that is grafted such as roses, passionfruit vines, natives and fruit trees. The rootstock leaves will look different to the top part of the plant; remove them as soon as they appear.

- Get enthused to plant out deciduous trees and shrubs for autumn colour. Most people plant out deciduous trees in winter, but you can select them now. You will need to think about the height you want and the width your tree will grow to. Many people fall in love with a particular tree only to find five years later that it's either far too big to fit in the area or too close to the house. Trees are the backbone and the main structure of any garden, so give time to pondering on which is the best species suited to your garden. If you visit your local nursery, they will have a good understanding of your soil type and know which trees do better in your area. Prepare the hole with everything bar the kitchen sink as the tree will be with you for many years and deserves a good start. Aged compost, slow-release fertiliser, water retention crystals, sheep poo, seaweed solution plus liquid fertiliser should all go into the hole before you plant out. It may seem like a lot of work, but you will be rewarded for your efforts within six months.

The edible garden

- Plant out autumn green manure crops in vegie beds. Try broad bean, lablab, mung bean, sub clover, vetch or mustard. They suppress weeds and fix nitrogen back into the soil.

- Asian greens will grow fast and if you sow now, you will get a harvest before the cold weather sets in. Try Chinese celery, mitsuba, mizuna, mustard greens, pak choy, perilla and tatsoi.
- Sow masses of English spinach and pick when it is very young. It tastes delicious and takes up very little room in the vegie patch.
- Water chestnuts will start dying down this month. Once the foliage has completely died down, they are ready to harvest.
- Apply 1 handful of rock dust per square metre to all the vegie beds and fruit trees.
- Don't apply too much nitrogen at this time of the year because it promotes soft leaf growth that may be affected by frost.
- Prune back by a third the new growth on apple and pear trees that have finished fruiting.
- Give citrus plants their final fertilising before winter. If the leaves are showing dark green veins on a yellowing leaf, spray the foliage with chelated iron.
- Spray grapevines with lime sulphur before leaf fall to kill pests and diseases harbouring in leaf tissue.

Natives

- Banksias and correas are in their full glory this month. There are many to choose from – nurseries can advise which are best suited to your soil type and climate. This is very important as many banksias are soil-specific and will not thrive if planted into the wrong climatic conditions. Correas are less fussy and come in splendid colours. Many do well in a shady spot. The small nectar-feeding birds love them.

- If you see galls on the leaves of wattle plants, these large swellings are caused by either a parasitic wasp or a borer. Prune off the affected branches and bin or burn.
- Apply iron chelates to any plant that has yellowing at the edges of the leaves. Native plants like grevillea and waxflower are especially susceptible.

Lawn

- Spike the lawn with a garden fork to help with drainage over winter rains.

Planting and cuttings

- Plant out flower seedlings that will provide you with colour over the winter months – pansy, primula, stock, cineraria, nemesia, violet, panola and cornflower.
- This is a good time of the year to plant annuals into hanging baskets. Pansies, violets and panolas are perfect for this and come in beautiful soft pastels and deep purples and blues.
- Use toilet roll tubes to start off your autumn seedlings.
- Allow some of your plants to go to seed for collection. Choose the healthiest and strongest plant and place a bag over it so the seed is not lost. Store in a glass jar and label.

Tropical/Subtropical

Edible garden tasks

- Sow Asian greens, basil, beetroot, broad beans, broccoli, carrot, cassava, celery, Chinese cabbage, chives, cress, daikon, dill, English spinach, French beans, garlic, kale, kohlrabi, leek, lettuce, mint, mustard, okra, potato, pumpkin, rocket, silverbeet, spring onion, swede, sweet corn, sweet potato, tomato.
- Keep planting out new strawberry runners into a mix of compost, manure and potting mix off the ground.
- Liquid-fertilise brassica plants (cabbage, broccoli, kale etc) to keep them forming up florets or strong new leaves.
- This is prime coriander time – it's about the only season that it doesn't immediately bolt to seed.
- Liquid-feed all vegies to keep them growing over the dry season.
- If you want beans to develop on your broad bean plants, spray the flowers with 1 teaspoon of sugar to 5 litres of water to attract the pollinators. Underplant with alyssum and thyme to keep and attract other insects.
- Get ready to plant potatoes (see pp. 75–8). Dig in lots of compost, manure and rock dust, turn it over and leave for 3 weeks before planting out disease-free certified potatoes.

- Pawpaw is fruiting and you can save the seeds and sow them into seed raising mix. Keep it moist but not too wet. Plant into bigger pots after 6 weeks or directly into the ground.
- Prepare fruit trees for the dry season. Apply a wetting agent if necessary and top up the mulch, making sure it doesn't come into contact with the trunk.
- Plant out some tropical fruit trees like custard apple, dragon fruit, mangosteen and Davidson's plum.
- Apply sulphate of potash around avocado, mango, star fruit and custard apple trees – it will help with flower set.
- Cabbage white butterflies will be attacking Asian greens and of course cabbage and other brassicas. Spray with Dipel or Success.
- Cassava, coffee, lemongrass and turmeric can be harvested now.

General garden tasks

- Plant out sweet peas (see pp. 40–2) into soil that has had a dressing of dolomite lime.
- Potted ferns will still require watering but their growth will slow down with the cooler nights. Move them into a more protected spot and liquid-fertilise half-strength once a month.
- Tip-prune rose bushes to keep flowers coming. Fertilise after pruning and mulch.

- Caladiums will be dying back now so it's a good time to dig them up, cut them right back and store the corms. Dust the cuts in powdered sulphur and store them in a cool, dark place until you replant.
- Cut off any scraggy bits left on ginger, heliconia and canna plants if you haven't already done so. Cut them to ground level, fertilise and replace the mulch.
- Divide up brachyscome daisy plants now and spread them around the garden. It's best to transplant immediately and give them a light trim.
- Prune yellow flowering conostylis back to the base of their flowering stems.

Temperate/Mediterranean

Edible garden tasks

- Sow artichoke, Asian greens, asparagus, broad beans, broccoli, celery, Chinese cabbage, chives, coriander, cress, daikon, dill, English spinach, Florence fennel, garlic, Jerusalem artichoke, kale, kohlrabi, leek, lettuce, mint, mustard, onion, parsley, peas, potato, radish, silverbeet, spring onion, swede.
- Vegies will grow very well in pots or bags in autumn. Get good quality potting mix, cocopeat and compost and mix together. Make sure there is enough drainage. Liquid-fertilise every fortnight.

- May is the perfect month to harvest your ginger and use the bulbs in cooking – they will be plump and full of flavour. Loosen the ground with a garden fork before pulling up the rhizomes. Leave some plants in the ground for next season. They will die down over winter but emerge again in spring. Fill the hole with compost and manure, drench with a seaweed solution or worm juice and wait for them to build up again.
- Prune back asparagus ferns to ground level and build up with compost and seaweed if you can get it – or pea straw, lupin or lucerne if you can't.
- Prune back female kiwifruit vines to below where the fruit formed. Male plants can be pruned to remove all the wood that's over one year old.
- Avoid direct sowing peas when you know it's going to rain heavily for several days in a row – they will rot in the ground if they get too wet.
- Fertilise winter-fruiting trees like kumquat, tamarillo and olive. Use a fertiliser that is for fruiting trees and has all the minerals needed to develop fruit. You can also use blood and bone, but add rock dust to make it a more complete fertiliser.

General garden tasks

- Give bearded iris a good feed before their display of flowers in a month's time. Make sure the fertiliser has magnesium and potassium. You can also use blood and bone with a teaspoon of Epsom salts and sulphate of potash.

- Plant out some gerberas into a sunny spot – the beneficial insects love them.
- Cut back perennials that have finished flowering, and tidy up dead leaves. Many will go into a dormant state over winter so they will not need fertilising until they resprout in the spring.
- Put snail traps around cymbidiums to keep the snails away from juicy flowering stems. You can also use pet-friendly snail pellets inside snail houses, or copper banding around the pots.
- Prune back biennial bedding begonias, cut back to 4 cm and give them a feed with a liquid fertiliser. Put snail beer traps around them to prevent new shoots being eaten.
- Cut back geraniums and pelargoniums that have become leggy or diseased. Never use the cuttings of any diseased plant – bag and bin.
- Gymea lilies may have seed pods ready for harvesting. Sow them into seed trays of seed raising mix and pot them up into individual pots when they are 4 cm long.
- Plant out November lilies for a lovely show in late spring and summer. They have a wonderful perfume and make great cut flowers for the house.
- Bulbs to plant now include tulip, hyacinth, Dutch iris, crocus, bluebell, daffodil and freesia. Corms to plant are anemone, ranunculus, sparaxis, babiana, tritonia, ipheion and ixia.
- Prune back hydrangeas, buddleias and callistemons that have finished flowering.

- Plant out annual flowers such as yarrow, candytuft, pansy, poppy, calendula and geum for a lovely winter display.

Cool/Cold

Edible garden tasks

- Sow artichoke, asparagus, broad beans, broccoli, brussels sprouts, cauliflower, celery, coriander, daikon, dill, endive, English spinach, garlic, Jerusalem artichoke, kale, leek, onion, parsley, radish, rhubarb, silverbeet, snow peas.
- Plant out brussels sprout seedlings. They will take about three months to develop sprout buds. They love the frosts and will form better sprouts after a good frosting. Brussels sprouts need full sun and soil with a pH of around 6.6–7.0. Plant them into freshly composted soil with a seaweed solution and mulch around the seedlings to retain moisture. Harvest them as they ripen. Heritage varieties will be ready from the bottom up.
- The growth rate of vegies will start to slow down. Keep applying a seaweed solution and worm juice to maintain health and vigour.
- If you have heavy clay soils you will need to improve drainage before the rains. Gypsum does not work on all soils. Construct drainage trenches to carry the water away. Plant onto mounds if plants are likely to be waterlogged in winter.

- Broad beans can be planted in rows 60 cm apart.
- Artichoke plants can be cut down to ground level.
- Leeks like slightly alkaline soils so add a handful of dolomite lime a week before planting seedlings out.
- Plant out a new herb garden. Many herbs are frost-hardy (except mint, basil and coriander) and will thrive at this time of the year.
- Plant out new raspberry bushes into well-drained, slightly acidic, compost-rich soil. It's worth doing the prep work as you will have the bushes providing you with delicious fruit for 25 years or more. Provide them with a trellis with 3 wires for support. Plant out in rows that run north to south. They will need protection from the hot afternoon sun. Build up mounds 10 cm high and plant out the bare-rooted stock into moist soil.
- Remove the old woody canes from raspberry plants and blackcurrant bushes. Leave the young green ones, which will bear next season's fruit. Tie the new canes to the trellis.
- Fertilise rhubarb plants and spread a layer of compost at the base of the plant. Start looking at rhubarb recipes in anticipation.

General garden tasks

- Divide up the ornamental alliums. Remove seed heads and sprinkle them around the garden.

- Prune back silver birch trees if they are badly shaped. You can create a bushier canopy or a taller thinner look.
- The nights will be getting much colder now and some areas may have already experienced frosts. Prepare for frosts by laying frost cloths over shrubs, trees and perennials that get affected. Mist-spraying the foliage at dawn helps minimise frost burn.
- Plant out the last of the bulbs such as daffodil, ranunculus, allium, lilium, peony, delphinium and lily-of-the-valley.
- Recycle 2-litre plastic milk or juice containers as a cloche to protect new seedlings from the cold. Remove them in the daytime if it's a nice sunny day and replace them late afternoon.
- Take hardwood cuttings from your rose, jasmine and honeysuckle plants. Place in a warm protected spot under cover. Plant out in late spring when they have developed a root system (see p. 203).
- Plant out bare-rooted lilacs – their fragrance is divine. They come in pink, blue, lilac, magenta and pure purple. They need a frost to flower really well and prefer alkaline soil, so add some dolomite lime at planting time.

June

Brassicas

Time to make a few changes and get those cold-season vegies in the garden. Brassicas planted now will get the chill they need to develop fully. The brassica family includes (among others) broccoli, brussels sprouts, cabbage, cauliflower, kale, kohlrabi, mustard and swede. Even wallflower and stock are in the brassica family – they all have a flower with four petals that form a cross.

These vegies like to grow with plenty of manure and compost that has been dug in a few weeks before planting. They are high nitrogen feeders and respond well to liquid fertiliser every two weeks.

Broccoli and broccolini are some of the fastest growing brassicas and need the nitrogen boost to form heads. Some gardeners use insect exclusion bags on the heads to ward off aphids, whitefly and the cabbage white butterfly. You will be harvesting within 12–16 weeks. Di Cicco Early and Romanesco are the most popular varieties.

Brussels sprouts are a very long term crop and need many frosts to develop the sprouts – you're looking at around 4–5 months before harvest. Long Island Improved is a shorter-growing variety that still produces 50–100 sprouts, and Red Ribs has beautiful nutty-flavoured sprouts.

Cabbages are great for the novice gardener to grow as you will get a harvest in 10–12 weeks and they will grow in a variety of climate zones – a frost is not needed.

They can also be planted out in a little shade. Cabbages can come in a variety of colours and crinkles these days. Red Drumhead, January King and Mini are great choices.

Cauliflower is another long-term crop – around the same as brussels sprouts – and has a similar chill requirement to form the curd (the white bit we eat). When the lower leaves have grown large enough, tie them at the top with a peg to cover the developing curd – it does not like being exposed to the sun. Try Green Macerata or, for a colour explosion, Purple Sicily. In cooler climates you can also grow Paleface. In warmer climates plant Snowball.

Kale is a great vegetable that seems to adapt to most soils and is a 'cut and come again' plant. Whitefly seem to like them too, unfortunately. There are so many varieties to choose from now like curly kale, red kale, black kale – and they are all delicious. You will be harvesting leaves in 3 weeks, along with the bugs that love them.

Brassicas' main pests are the dreaded whitefly, the cabbage white butterfly and aphids.

Control whitefly with pyrethrum or botanical oil.

For the cabbage white butterfly, some gardeners swear by leaving plastic cut-outs of the butterfly on the ends of sticks to deter them – they are very territorial and this is meant to hold them at bay. The caterpillars can be sprayed with Dipel or Success, which use a naturally occurring bacteria that affects caterpillars but doesn't harm anything else.

Aphids can be controlled with Beat-a-Bug, Natrasoap, Eco-Oil or pyrethrum.

Pollination

Most of us don't think about pollen, except when we have lilies in a vase and the pollen hanging on the anthers stains everything it touches. We all know that pollination is required in plants to make fruit, but we know little about how pollen actually works. As we head out to nurseries to buy our deciduous fruit trees and berry bushes, there are a few things we need to know about how trees pollinate.

There are two different types of pollination: *self-pollination*, where pollen is transferred from the anther to the stigma on the same flower, and *cross-pollination*, where two parent plants with different genetic constitutions transfer the pollen from the anther on one plant to the stigma on another. Many fruit trees that need a partner pollinator come into the latter category. (See more in 'Partnering up for fruiting success', pp. 117–19.)

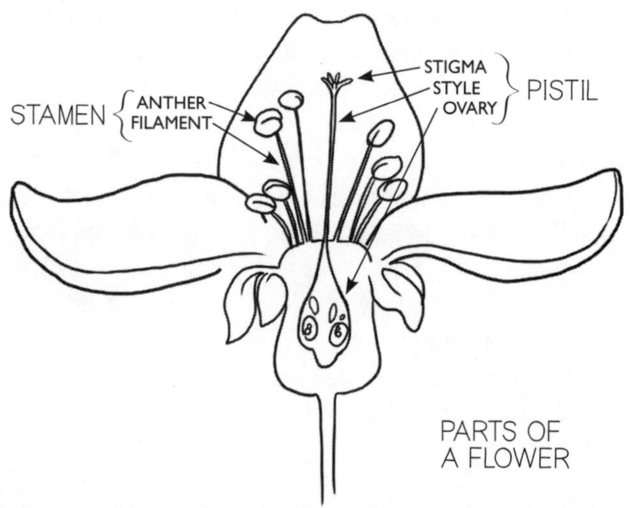

Self-pollination

Self-pollination is self-explanatory. Everything that's needed for pollination is contained within the flower, which means we can sit down, relax and have a glass of wine while the plant does it all itself.

There are three types of self-pollination:

1. Transfer of pollen from the anther to the stigma within the same flower. Examples are wheat, barley and peas.
2. Transfer of pollen from the anther to the stigma of other flowers on the same plant. This happens in tomatoes, potatoes, apricots and peaches.
3. Transfer of pollen from the anther to the stigma of flowers that come from genetically identical plants.

Cross-pollination

Cross-pollination always involves two plants that have a different genetic makeup. The two plants can be the same species, different species and even different genera. Cross-pollination requires wind, water, insects or other animals to transfer the pollen to other flowers. Apples, plums, pears, raspberries, pumpkin and lavender are a few examples of insect-pollinated plants. Grasses, she-oaks, corn and dandelions are examples of wind-pollinated plants.

Insect pollination requires the plant to expend energy on attracting insects. Plants usually have larger flowers with brightly coloured petals; they produce nectar and perfume, and have elongated stamens and pistils to lure insects in. Some orchids actually mimic the female wasp to entice the male wasp into their pollen-laden flowers.

Some plants are capable of self-pollination but have extraordinary methods of preventing it. A good example is avocados. Although they produce millions of flowers, the amount of fruit set is relatively small.

The flower is complete, meaning it has both the male and the female parts in the one flower. The tricky part is that the flower opens and closes twice over a two-day cycle, first as a female, then as a male.

Avocados have one of two flowering sequences: type A opens up as female on day one, closes in the afternoon, then reopens on the afternoon of day two as male before closing again. Type B opens as female in the afternoon of day one, closes, then reopens as male in the morning of day two before closing again.

To make things even more impossible for self-pollination, the flowers are all synchronised in their sex when they open. You would think this is an evolutionary glitch, but the purpose is to increase genetic diversity by cross-pollinating with a different tree. You need an avocado tree from group A and one from group B to get the timing right when the boys are in the same playground as the girls.

So if you are not getting any joy from your avocado, now you know why. Seems a terrible waste of energy producing all those flowers, but in a forest there's lots of diversity to choose from – far more than an urban back yard can produce.

An area that receives little research or media coverage is the number of plant species that rely on animals other than European bees for pollination. Bees seem to be getting all the publicity, but our own native flora is highly dependent on animals to transfer pollen from one plant to another.

Australian flora and fauna have evolved together and the increasing practice of land clearing for human development and land use for mining is having a devastating effect on pollinator communities because of the disappearance of plant species.

In saying that, Australia still has over 200,000 species of animals that act as pollen vectors, most of them insects like beetles, bees, ants, wasps, butterflies and moths.

Many small mammals are vital to the genetic diversity of Australian flora. The pygmy possum and honey possum pollinate the flowers of banksia and eucalypt species. They have grasping feet and a prehensile tail that helps them hang in the tree's flowers, drinking the nectar with a very long tongue designed for that purpose. The pollen transfer is unnoticed. Land clearing and feral predation are significantly affecting the numbers of our smaller marsupials, so I hope they will still be here in fifty years.

The shape of a flower usually relates to the behaviour of the pollinator. Plants produce flowers with landing pads, elongated pistils for hovering insects or tubes for honeyeater beaks to dive into. Bats and moths also feed on nectar-rich flowers, which are usually white, highly perfumed at night and occur on isolated branches away from masses of stems and leaves so bats don't become tangled in the growth.

Evolution is clever, and pollen under an electron microscope is a beautiful thing. Let's never take it for granted – without pollen we would all starve.

Pest watch

Snails and slugs will be laying eggs in the top 5 cm of soil, so go out and watch them at night. Apply the blundie boot method to prevent the next generation appearing.

Citrus bud mite causes severely distorted fruit. The mites feed on the unopened flower and leaf buds of your citrus trees. The fruit looks like it has grown fingers and the leaves will be curved and twisted. Spray the trees in June with sulphur to kill the mites that are beneath the buds.

All regions

General care

- Take some time to watch nature and observe the changes in your garden. The sun sits lower in the sky and the changes in light give the garden a whole different feel. Some parts of the garden that received sunlight may now be in partial or full shade over the winter months. Hopefully all but the tropical regions have received some rain by now and the ground will be soft and moist.
- On the subject of rain: garden beds that are under eaves may be sheltered from the rain and will dry out quickly; you may need to supplement watering by hand if this is the case.
- Check all mulch around plants to make sure the precious rainwater is getting through to the subsoil. If not, apply a wetting agent and break up the mulch.
- The terrible lawn prickle bindii will start making a presence. It's better to remove or spray the weeds when they are small, before they set seed. They look like miniature carrot leaves.
- Start up the winter compost heap. Make sure you have a bale of hay nearby to bulk up the carbon content and prevent it from getting too wet. (See more on pp. 25–7.)
- Remove rootstock suckers from grafted trees and vines by ripping them off. Otherwise the rootstock will take over the plant you paid a lot of money for.

Natives

- Cut banksia flowers to bring indoors. They last for ages in a vase and this is a better way of pruning them back.

Lawn

- Aerate the lawn and garden beds with a strong garden fork to alleviate any waterlogging.

Pruning

- Sharpen up the pruning tools and run linseed oil into wooden handles of gardening tools. Sharp blades mean less work for the pruner and less chance of tearing bark.
- Prune back poinsettias that have finished with their display of red bracts.
- Remove selected branches from trees if you want more light coming through. Do not chop stems halfway down as this encourages thicker growth. Remove them at the trunk.

Planting and cuttings

- Plant out the spring-flowering seeds like larkspur, nemesia, cosmos, candytuft and hollyhock.
- Tubestock plants will respond with loads of growth when planted out in winter rains. Soak them before planting.

- Soak all bare-rooted plants in a liquid seaweed solution prior to planting to ease transplant shock.
- Lift and divide native iris (*Patersonia*) making sure there is some root in each piece. Replant them into pots to get more established before planting out into the garden.

Tropical/Subtropical

Edible garden tasks

- Sow Asian greens, asparagus, basil, beetroot, broad beans, broccoli, carrot, celery, Chinese cabbage, chives, coriander, cress, English spinach, Florence fennel, French beans, garlic, kale, kohlrabi, leek, lettuce, mint, mustard, okra, potato, pumpkin, silverbeet, spring onion, sweet corn, sweet potato, tomato.
- Asian greens and lettuce can be grown in pots that can be moved around the garden to find adequate amounts of sunshine.
- Tomato plants will need to be watered regularly in order to prevent blossom-end rot.
- Garlic can be chilled in the crisper of the fridge for a couple of weeks to induce shooting before planting into improved soil.
- Prune two-year-old asparagus to ground level. Top up with compost and lupin hay and water in well.
- Pineapples have started developing flowers and will need fertilising. Use an organic-based fertiliser.

- Keep hilling up around sweet corn and check for budworm that bores holes into the cobs.
- Give a light prune to passionfruit vines by cutting back long twining laterals by a third. Apply a dressing of sulphate of potash.
- Mulch all vegie beds and deep-water any trees. Bare-rooted deciduous fruit trees are available now for planting, but keep in mind some fruiting trees need a pollinator – they will not bear fruit without a partner to cross-pollinate (see pp. 117–19). Find out the chill factor of plants so that you purchase one that's suitable for your climate zone – they will either be high-chill (needing many nights of temperatures below 7.2 degrees) or low-chill (needing only a small amount of winter chill).
- Spray all deciduous fruit trees with lime sulphur or copper hydroxide to kill any pests under leaves and reduce the incidence of peach leaf curl.
- Fertilise pawpaws with trace elements mixed in water and sprayed on the foliage.
- Tamarind pods will be filling up nicely. Wait until the pods are dry before harvesting.
- Protect ripening figs from the birds with wildlife-friendly netting that is white and densely woven, to prevent the birds from becoming entangled.

General garden tasks

- Although it's no longer hot, it is dry. Make sure the garden, especially fruit trees, is receiving enough water and top up the mulch in all garden beds.
- Weeds may invade your garden beds. A good, thick mulch should prevent them from taking over. Make sure you cut the heads off weeds before they flower or you will have many more.
- Divide and replant hippeastrum and day lilies into improved soil. Check for thrips and scale.
- Prune fuchsias and use prunings for cuttings to make new plants.
- Prune hydrangeas to double-flowering buds and spray with wettable sulphur. Use the prunings for cuttings to make new plants. Pot them up into a propagation mix and leave in a sheltered spot out of the sun.
- Lightly prune abelia and sasanqua camellias that have finished flowering.

Temperate/Mediterranean

Edible garden tasks

- Sow artichoke, asparagus, broad beans, broccoli, Chinese cabbage, chives, cress, dill, endive, English spinach, garlic, Jerusalem artichoke, kale, kohlrabi, lettuce, mint, mustard, onion, parsley, peas, radish, swede.

- June is the best month to select and plant out bare-rooted fruit trees. Make sure you purchase the trees that are suitable to the chill factor in your area (see p. 104), and consider their pollination needs (see pp. 117–19).
- The best fruiting trees to plant now are the English mulberry, quince, apple, pear, nectarine, plum and apricot.
- Spray all fruit trees with copper oxychloride, Kocide or Bordeaux to prevent fungal and bacterial diseases that will emerge in spring.
- Spray citrus trees with Eco-Oil to prevent damage by the bronze orange bug nymphs. Nymphs are much easier to control than the adult bugs.
- Use the finger squishing technique on any aphids that attack new growth on citrus trees and cut out any swollen lumps caused by the citrus gall wasp.
- Prune back apple trees, removing a third of all growth. Remove any diseased or weak branches and spray with either copper hydroxide or Kocide.
- Grapevines can be pruned from this month. Cut back to short, 3-bud spurs at 20 cm intervals along the stems of old wood. Remove the wood and destroy. After pruning, spray the vines with a botanical oil or pest oil.
- Plant out rhubarb crowns into a sunny spot. Prepare the ground a few weeks before with sheep poo and compost. Mulch after planting with lupin or pea hay.

- Divide clumps of lemongrass after giving them a hard prune. The edges of the leaves are extremely sharp so you will need to wear tough gloves. Cut off all the old dead growth down to ground level. Remaining foliage can be cut back by half and side clumps lifted and replanted.

General garden tasks

- Pull back on the watering of indoor and potted plants. Their growth rate will have slowed right down.
- Winter weeds are emerging with the rains. Hand-pull them before they get established and set seed.
- Apply 1 handful per sqm of dolomite lime to lawns. It helps control moss and feeds the grass magnesium.
- Time to prune back your deciduous trees, shrubs and perennials. Leave the roses for another month, until after the threat of frosts. When pruning trees think about the overall shape and make sure you leave a good structure in place for the years to come.
- Large clumps of ornamental grasses can be cut right back. If it's easier to do it with a whipper-snipper that's fine. Rake up the prunings and bin.
- Hellebores will be budding up for their winter blooming. Even without the flowers the foliage is spectacular. Give them a liquid feed with an organic-based fertiliser with added minerals.

- The sweet perfume of daphne will be filling the air. Plant them out into camellia and azalea potting mix or into improved soil with added slow-release fertiliser. In warmer climates grow them in morning sun only, but cooler climates can grow them as a hedging plant.
- Plant summer-flowering bulbs like tuberose, valotta and lilium.
- Plant out flowering annuals such as delphinium, foxglove, poppy, primula, wallflower, stock and viola.
- Take hardwood cuttings from deciduous shrubs and pot up into propagation mix. Keep protected from the cold.

Cool/Cold

Edible garden tasks

- Sow artichoke, asparagus, broad beans, broccoli, brussels sprouts, carrot, cauliflower, endive, English spinach, garlic, Jerusalem artichoke, onion, radish, snow peas.
- June is the best month to select and plant out bare-rooted fruit trees. Make sure you purchase the trees that are suitable to the chill factor in your area (see p. 104), and consider their pollination needs (see pp. 117–19).
- Angelica, Florence fennel, chervil and lovage are some of the more unusual crops that do well in cooler climates. Plant them out into compost-enriched soil. Frosts won't bother them.

- This is the latest to be planting out broad bean seeds into a bed that has had dolomite lime and compost dug in two weeks previously.
- Put corrugated cardboard or hessian traps at the base of apple trees to capture the grubs of codling moths – they will nest inside.
- Plant out dwarf varieties of apples and pears into large pots. Rake up all leaves and twigs.
- Thin out fruiting spurs in pear trees, leaving 15 cm between spurs.
- Select Japanese flowering cherries and laburnums for planting now – the spring display is breathtaking.

General garden tasks

- Cold winds can dry the soil out very quickly; check that moisture levels are adequate for evergreens.
- Give rhododendrons and daphnes a dose of Epsom salts to keep them green over winter.
- Make cloches for vegetable seedlings and move tender plants into a more sheltered position. Cover plants with cloth or mesh to save them from frost burn. Mist-spray early in the morning to melt ice crystals off leaf tissue.
- If you are in frost-prone areas and have a small pond, float a tennis ball near the centre – it will absorb some of the pressure caused by the formation of ice crystals.

- Don't waste all the fallen ornamental deciduous leaves. They make great mulch for garden beds, preventing winter weeds from taking over. Apply a sparing sprinkle of blood and bone to help them break down quickly.
- Hellebores will be flowering and growing well in winter. After flowering some will drop seeds and the seedlings can be moved and replanted to form great clumps.
- Protect young plants against the ravages of strong winter winds by putting up a shade cloth barrier around three strong stakes.
- Divide perennial asters and shasta daisies. Cut them back hard and replant into composted soil.

July

Rose pruning

Climate creep is certainly affecting the way we garden. Winters are starting later, summers are longer and the distinction between spring and summer, and autumn and winter is almost lost. Basically gardeners can now move lots of jobs forward at least a month. A good example of changing garden practices is the timing of pruning – not just fruit trees but roses too.

Traditionally roses were pruned any time from June in frost-free areas, but now with the extended warm weather, roses are still blooming in June and frosts are still around in August and September. In response we need to prune our roses at the end of July or in August. This is great news for gardeners who never seem to get around to doing chores in the garden – mark it in your calendar to prune in June and by August you will get around to it.

If you live in an area that gets frosts, leave rose pruning until the end of August. You don't want new growth burnt by frost as these will be your new flowering stems.

The one important exception to pruning a rose at this time of the year is the non-repeat flowering roses that flower only in spring – do not prune these in winter as you are pruning off all the flowering stems.

Do we really need to prune roses? Well, if you want healthy plants that give lots of flowers, yes you do. The flowers are formed on new growth that's less than one year old. Novice gardeners are usually terrified of pruning their rose bushes, but it's better to hack away than not to prune at all. Thankfully, roses are pretty tough customers and are forgiving of the bad short back and sides.

Courage and practice are all that's needed – and a bit of information to help you get through the first pruning sessions.

You will need some protective armour, long sleeves, good strong gloves, secateurs, long-handled loppers, a curved pruning saw, something to mop up the blood and some disinfectant on standby. Use sharp secateurs – it is far less frustrating than having to grind a stem off.

So where to begin? For the majority of roses you can take off 50 per cent of the growth. This may seem a lot when you look at the few remaining stems but, believe me, they love it. Take out any branches in the centre, crossing branches or diseased wood.

After pruning, remove any leaves still on the bush and spray with a copper or lime sulphur spray to kill off mites and fungal spores. The bush should look clean and have outward-facing stems that are pruned off just above an outward-facing bud.

Hybrid Tea Roses

1. Prune every branch back by 50 per cent. Now you can actually see the bush.
2. Prune off all the older stems at ground level and take out any stems that are in the middle of the bush.

ROSE PRUNING

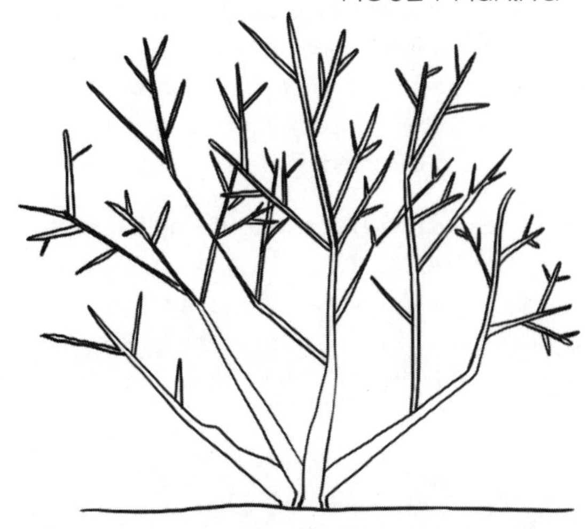

A MODERATE PRUNE

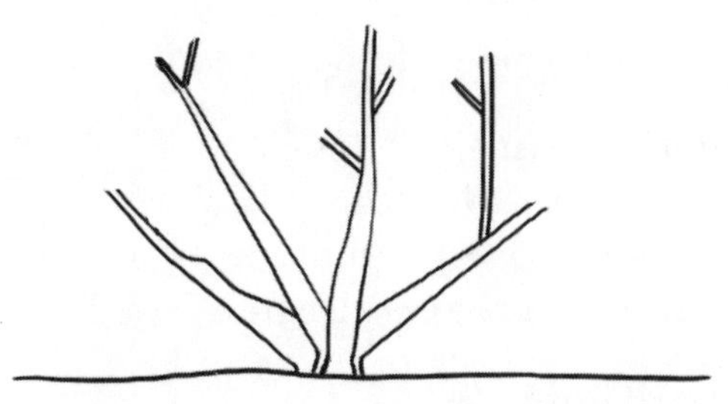

A HARDER PRUNE

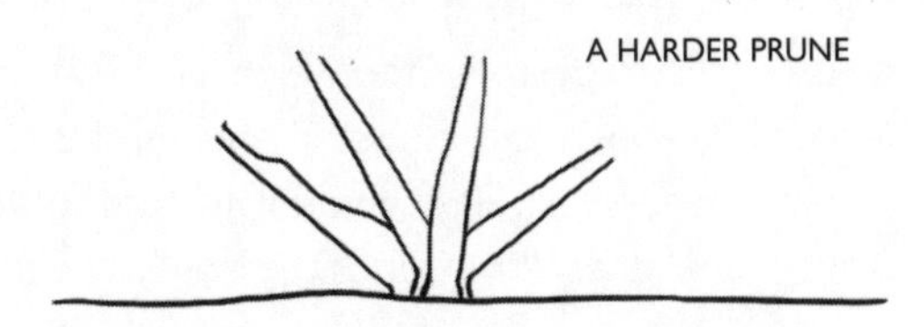

3. With the secateurs, prune back all but five stems to an outward-facing bud, leaving only one branch coming off that, again to an outward-facing bud.
4. Spray with a copper or lime sulphur spray to reduce overwintering fungal spores.

Shrub Roses – David Austin and English roses

1. Prune back the whole bush by one-third and take out any stems that are in the middle of the bush.
2. Remove any dead wood at the base of the plant and any branches that are more than three years old.
3. Cut back remaining stems (leave no more than nine stems) to ground level.
4. Prune back remaining branches to an outward-facing bud.
5. Spray with a copper or lime sulphur spray to reduce overwintering fungal spores.

Floribunda Roses

These are pruned much the same as hybrid tea roses but take one-third off rather than one half, and you can leave more stems coming from the base.

Standard Roses

These are just hybrid tea or floribunda roses that are grafted on a long stem. It is very important to prune these each year to decrease the weight of the head. Many a standard has been lost in a storm when the top part has simply snapped off, leaving you with bare rootstock.

You prune it as for hybrid tea roses and remove

any growth that sprouts below the graft. Make sure it is equally balanced with even branching on all sides.

Weeping Standard Roses

I think I have seen the worst massacred roses in this category. Please don't prune your weeping standard into a mini-skirt or a trimmed grass tree; they look ridiculous.

1. Remove at least 50 per cent of the oldest canes from the very base of the standard.
2. Prune off all the side shoots from the remaining canes but do not shorten them.
3. Stand back and check if you need to remove any more canes.
4. The remaining canes should have all the side shoots pruned off to just above ground level.
5. Spray with a copper or lime sulphur spray to reduce overwintering fungal spores.

Climbing Roses

Climbing roses are a bit different to prune. They have several main branches, and secondary stems coming from these that produce the flowers.

The good thing for novice gardeners is that you don't need to prune climbing roses for the first few years – just train the canes where you want them to grow.

1. Remove one-third of the oldest canes at the base of the plant. You can remove the oldest canes once they are a few years old to encourage new watershoots, which are the purple-coloured soft stems that emerge from the base.

2. Prune back the side shoots coming off these canes to two buds. Remove any twiggy or thin growth.
3. Tie remaining canes in a curved horizontal position to encourage more flowering stems.
4. Spray with a copper or lime sulphur spray to reduce overwintering fungal spores.

Miniature Roses

Miniature roses are great to prune. All you need is a pair of shears and to have had a bad day. You can rip into them with gusto, not even looking where the shears are going, and you can swear at the same time. Very therapeutic to get all the anger out and the joy of gardening back in.

Handy Hints

- Non-repeat flowering roses that have their main big flush in spring, such as the banksia rose, should *not* be pruned now. It's best to prune them after flowering finishes at the end of spring.
- It is important to sterilise your pruning tools after each rose bush. This will prevent fungal diseases being transferred from one rose bush to another. You can spray the tools with methylated spirits, diluted bleach or tea-tree oil.

Partnering up for fruiting success

There is a lot of confusion around which fruit trees need partners in order to cross-pollinate and produce fruit. The pollination section on pp. 96–100 will give you the basics of self-pollination versus cross-pollination. But here we take the next step by looking at the specific needs of common fruit trees in the garden.

Some trees, such as citrus, are self-fertile. Others, like certain avocados, are partially self-fertile. Then there are those, such as apples and plums, that need a different variety that flowers at the same time in order to develop fruit.

Most nurseries that sell fruit trees will have labels advising the suitable pollinator plant for that variety.

Self-pollinating fruit trees (meaning you only need one tree)

All citrus, most figs, apricot, banana, elderberry, guava, loganberry, loquat, lychee, mango, medlar, mulberry, nectarine, peach, pomegranate and quince.

Partially self-pollinating fruit trees (meaning it can fruit with only one tree, but often does better with two)

Cherry (Stella and Sunburst), feijoa and astringent persimmons.

Avocado (Hass, Fuerte and Reed) could also be included on this list as long as you have plenty of bees around to do the pollinating for you. (For more on avocado and pollination see p. 98.)

Pollinator required (meaning you need two different trees that flower at the same time)

Almond, apple, carob, cherry, lychee, pawpaw, pear, plum, sapote and non-astringent persimmon.

Apples

Variety	Pollinators
Cox Orange Pippin	Jonathan, Granny Smith
Crimson Crisp	Jonathan, Granny Smith, Pixie Crunch
Gala	Granny Smith, Pink Lady, Red Delicious, Red Fuji
Golden Delicious	Granny Smith, Jonathan, Red Fuji, Red Delicious
Lady William	Jonathan, Golden Delicious, Granny Smith
Leprechaun	Pinkabelle, Gala, Golden Delicious, Red Delicious, Jonathan
Monty's Surprise	Pinkabelle, Gala, Golden Delicious, Red Delicious, Leprechaun
Pink Lady	Gala, Red Delicious, Pixie Crunch, Crimson Crunch
Pinkabelle	Gala, Golden Delicious, Red Delicious, Leprechaun, Jonathan

Pears

Variety	Pollinators
Beurre Bosc	Nijisseiki, Williams, Sensation
Josephine	Packham
Nashi Chojuro	Nijisseiki

Nashi Kosui	Williams
Packham	Josephine
Pipsqueak	self-pollinating
Sensation	Beurre Bosc, Nashi Kosui
Williams	Beurre Bosc

Plums

Variety	**Pollinators**
Flavour Rouge	Mariposa, can be self-pollinating
Gulf Ruby	Sunrise Gulf, Santa Rosa
Marcia's Flavour	self-pollinating
Narrabeen	Mariposa, Santa Rosa, Satsuma
Pizazz	Mariposa, Flavour Supreme
Ruby Blood	Mariposa, Santa Rosa, Narrabeen, Wickson
Santa Rosa	Mariposa
Satsuma	Mariposa, Santa Rosa, Narrabeen, Ruby Blood

There are many nurseries that specialise in fruit trees where you can obtain all the information on selecting the right tree for your climate, soil type and size of garden. Bear in mind some fruit varieties are better suited to specific chill factors so be sure to check whether they need a sustained cold winter (high chill) or milder winters with few nights below 7.2 degrees (low chill).

Pest watch

Bronze orange bug will be hatching. The eggs, laid in midsummer, are interesting – the adult bug lays around 15 eggs in 4 rows on the underside of citrus leaves. The green, oval-shaped nymphs emerge in winter and are 6 mm long with flat bodies. As they age, they turn bright orange with a black spot, then brown with a shiny sheen, eventually growing to 25 mm long and turning almost black. Adults and nymphs suck the sap from the stalk of the flower, causing fruit and flower fall.

Because they cluster in groups, you can knock them off into a bucket of soapy water. Always wear gloves and a long-sleeved shirt to protect you from the caustic liquid they squirt as a defence mechanism. On really hot days the bugs will harbour at the base of citrus trees, making it easy to collect them and bucket them. I use tongs to pick them up from the ground – just don't put the tongs back in the kitchen drawer.

Spray the trees with Eco-Oil or Eco-Neem to kill both adults and nymphs.

All regions

General care

- If you have winter rains the soil may be depleted of nutrients and become either too acid or alkaline. You can apply liquid gypsum and dolomite lime for acid soils, but never use it at the same time as spreading fresh animal manure – ammonia gas will be released, which has a detrimental effect on plant roots, particularly those of annual vegetables.

- Spray camellias with a horticultural oil like Eco-Oil to control camellia mite and scale.
- Make sure succulents are receiving enough light and are not being overwatered. Allow them to dry out before watering.

The edible garden

- Mid July is the best time to give all fruit trees a spray with a pest oil like Eco-Oil or PestOil. This thin layer of oil smothers mites and scale that would otherwise become a major problem in spring. Oils are better used in the cooler months.
- Spray all deciduous fruit trees with a copper-based fungicide like Kocide to help control peach leaf curl, shothole, bacterial canker and downy mildew.
- Spray grapevines with wettable sulphur to prevent the development of powdery mildew. If you have had persistent problems with powdery mildew, switch to lime sulphur while it's dormant and then back to wettable sulphur once the vine shoots leaves and flowers. Lime sulphur will burn the flowers. This spray will also help to control leaf blister mite, which emerges at bud burst.

- Harvest citrus daily. Make sure branches weighed down with fruit don't touch the ground, as that will cause fungal diseases in the fruit.

Natives

- Transplant small native seedlings that have popped up in the garden.
- Keep planting out tubestock of native plants. There will still be rain around and the soil will be moist. Make sure mulch is not too thick, allowing winter rains to penetrate the ground.

Lawn

- Control bindii prickles in lawns before they seed. You can hand-weed them out when they are small but if you have an infestation you may need to spray with a specific bindii herbicide.

Pruning

- This is the time of year when some serious pruning can be carried out on deciduous trees and vines where you need new fruiting wood to form. Fruit trees such as apples, apricots, pears and plums may only need pruning every second year. The great thing about winter pruning is the trees are bare and you can see the whole structure of the tree, making it easier to navigate around the branches.

- Prune and divide perennials such as aster, yarrow, rudbeckia and dianthus.
- Prune back poinsettias by 50 per cent, being careful not to get the sap on your skin or in your eyes. Dispose of the prunings in the bin, or start new plants from cuttings.

Planting and cuttings

- Sasanqua camellias can be transplanted at this time of the year. Give them a light prune and plant into slightly acidic soil.
- Plant out bare-rooted roses. Soak the roots in a seaweed solution before putting into the ground.
- Prune tree dahlias to ground level and use the hardwood prunings for cuttings. Lay them horizontally into propagation mix and just press down.
- Propagate brugmansia cuttings in the same method as tree dahlias.

Tropical/Subtropical

Edible garden tasks

- Sow artichoke, Asian greens, asparagus, basil, beetroot, broad beans, broccoli, carrot, celery, Chinese cabbage, chives, choko, coriander, English spinach, French beans, garlic, lettuce, melon, mint, mustard, okra, parsley, potato, pumpkin, radish, rocket, silverbeet, spring onion, sweet corn, sweet potato, tomato.

- Spray mango trees if you see evidence of thrips. Use potassium soap or neem oil.
- Deep-water all your fruit trees. July is a very windy and dry month, so make sure you have the mulch topped up to a depth of 5 cm.
- Spray pawpaw trees with wettable sulphur to prevent powdery mildew developing in the hotter months. Make sure you cover the backs of leaves and the trunk as this will also control mites.
- Give all custard apple trees a handful of sulphate of potash to help them fight anthracnose disease.
- Pineapple plants will start to colour up in the centre. Apply some blood and bone around the base to encourage further growth.
- Harvest baby kohlrabi, parsnips and new baby potatoes.
- Finish pruning grapevines this month. There will be very little sap flow and the vines won't bleed too much. If your vines are disease-free you can grow new plants from the cuttings, but remove excess prunings away from the main vine.
- Make sure mulch is well away from the trunks of citrus trees to discourage collar rot.
- Make an asparagus bed and plant crowns. They are a very long-lived plant so it is better to give them their own area as they tend to spread quickly. Crowns should be around 6 cm under the ground. Cover with pea straw, lupin or lucerne. (See more on pp. 42–4.)

General garden tasks

- Keep the compost heap moist by watering every week with a seaweed solution.
- Getting into the garden during these cooler months is so rewarding. Brighten the garden up with flowering annuals such as pansy, marigold, candytuft, cosmos and cornflower.
- Watch the birds flock to the tropical flowering grevilleas to get their daily fix of nectar. Place a birdbath near larger grevilleas so they can bathe in the morning.
- Similarly, fill birdbaths or shallow dishes of water for frogs, birds, lizards and beneficial insects during the dry season.
- Take cuttings of frangipani. Leave them to dry out for 10 days before potting up into potting mix.
- Many grevilleas and banksias will be in flower. Visit nurseries now – they will have a large selection to choose from to suit every size garden.
- Prune abelia and elderberry bushes.
- Control budworm in corn, on tomato fruit and on mango flowers with a caterpillar-specific spray like Dipel or Success.
- Allow caladiums to die down and do not water until they come out of dormancy.

Temperate/Mediterranean

Edible garden tasks

- Sow artichoke, asparagus, broccoli, carrot, Chinese cabbage, chives, coriander, cress, dill, endive, English spinach, garlic, Jerusalem artichoke, kale, lettuce, mint, mustard, onion, parsley, parsnip, peas, radish, rocket.
- Persimmon and loquat trees can have a light prune to allow airflow and sunlight into the centre of the tree. Thin out loquat fruit by about a third (if you have parrots this will be done for you).
- Flowering peaches, plums and cherries will be budding up now ready to burst into spring. Apply a liquid potassium spray to the entire tree to help the trees hold on to the flowers.
- Japanese flowering quince will be in bloom now, so it's the right time to identify non-flowering wood. Mark these branches with a tie and prune them off when the quince has finished flowering.

General garden tasks

- Check underneath mulch after rainfall to make sure the water is soaking into the ground. If the mulch is too deep it might absorb all the water before it gets to plant roots.
- If you have a bore or drip line reticulation that is turned off during the winter months you will

need to run it once a month to keep the lines clear of insects, soil and plant roots. This also applies to greywater systems.

- Tropical plants may show signs of yellowing in winter months. This is normal because of colder temperatures. They will not be actively growing so there is no point in fertilising yet – wait until the nights warm up and the daylight hours become longer.
- There are lots of plants that bear pretty berries at this time of the year. Choose from ardisia, nandina, pistachio, hawthorn, blueberry ash, lilly pilly and euonymus.
- The orange trumpet vine (*Pyrostegia venusta*) will be in its full glory but has the ability to take over entire sheds. Wait for flowering to finish and give it a hard prune.
- This is the time to choose banksia plants as they will be coming into flower with their beautiful cones. Banksias are very soil-specific so only grow the ones that are suitable for your soil type and climate. Western Australian banksias do not like heavy wet soil just as Queensland and New South Wales coastal banksias hate Western Australia's sandy alkaline coastal sands.
- Transplant cycads from pots to a protected place in the garden. Give them a deep watering the day before transplanting and do the same with the hole that the cycad is going into. When transplanting you will need to wear strong

protective gloves and make clean cuts to the root system with secateurs. With a small paintbrush dab the root ends with powdered sulphur. Do not water for three days after transplanting as the wounds must heal first.

Cool/Cold

Edible garden tasks

- Sow artichoke, asparagus, broad beans, broccoli, coriander, endive, English spinach, garlic, Jerusalem artichoke, mint, onion, peas, radish, snow peas.
- This is the prime time to sow long-keeping onions like Brown, Spanish and Creamgold in soil that has had a dressing of dolomite lime. Choose a spot where onions haven't grown for the past five years to avoid problems with diseases. (See crop rotation on pp. 54–7.) Make sure the area is weed-free – this is the greatest problem for onion growers. Good companion plants are carrot, beetroot and chamomile.
- Apply a dressing of sulphate of potash to broad beans to keep them flowering.
- Plant out grapes, kiwifruit, hazelnut, pistachio, almond and pecan trees.
- Tie down leaders of fruit trees and apply sulphate of potash. Give them a light dressing of compost.
- Apply Kocide or copper oxychloride to all bare stone fruit trees to help control against brown rot.

- Plum trees that refuse to fruit can have their outer roots chopped with a spade or mattock. This will initiate flowering in the spring.
- Prune nectarine and peach trees, taking out weak growth on any branches that have fruited this year. Prune back long stems by a third.

General garden tasks

- Spray an anti-transpirant like DroughtShield on vulnerable plants to protect them from frost. In very cold areas, make a tent from hessian or other cloth to protect the entire plant until after the last frost. Do not prune any damaged tissue until the threat of frosts is over.
- Apply good quality blood and bone to native plants. Read the bag to make sure it's not filled out with urea as this will kill natives. The heavier the bag the more bone meal it has in it, which is a great source of slow-release phosphorus.
- Divide chrysanthemum plants and give them a liquid feed.
- Shape deciduous ornamental trees so they have a good balance of branches and remove any dead wood. It is better to remove entire branches than chop them off halfway, which makes them too top heavy and prevents sunlight from entering the tree.
- Plant out lily-of-the-valley and peony into improved soil. Add compost and leaf mulch from deciduous trees.

- Rearrange the tool shed and make new areas to store seeds. Glass jars are ideal for seed storage – they are safe from insect attack and keep dry.

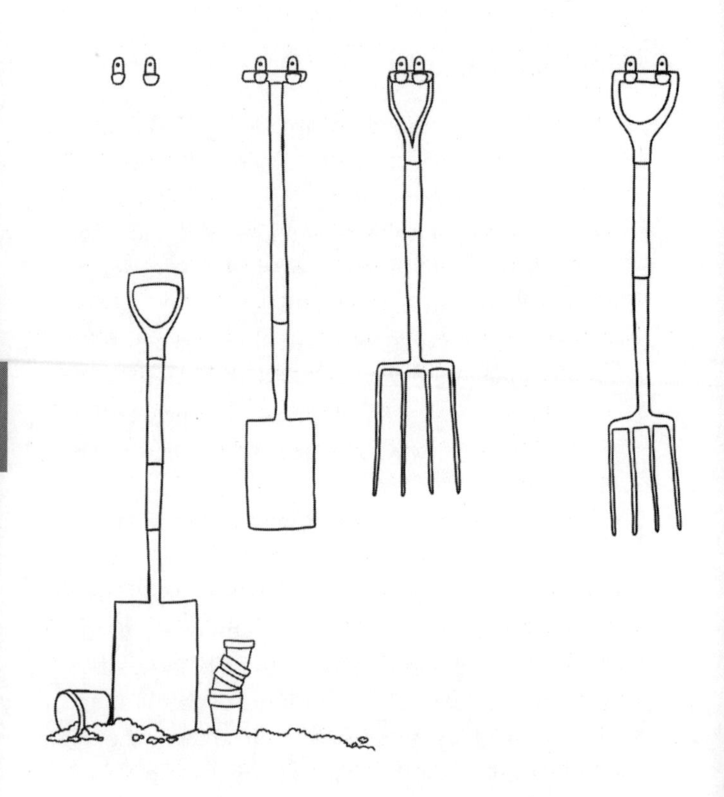

August

Blueberries

I get so excited when I wander around the garden and see little fruiting buds swelling up. Even more so when it's the blueberries about to pop.

In order to get the longest season and the most berries, you need to get a few different varieties. There are lots to choose from, but make sure you get the bushes that are best suited to your climate.

Basically, blueberries are divided into three categories: Northern Highbush, Southern Highbush and Rabbiteye. Northern Highbush are known as the high-chill varieties – they require 800 hours of chill. Southern Highbush cultivars require only 300 hours. The Rabbiteye, from the south of the US, require the least amount of chill.

I strongly recommend growing blueberries in pots if you live in impoverished alkaline soils, but they can be grown in the ground if you are blessed with good soil that is rich in humus and retains moisture. They certainly don't like the extreme summer heat, so in pots you can move them into dappled light or afternoon shade as the months warm up.

Camellia and azalea potting mix is ideal with added compost and manure. If they are grown in pots be careful with the fertiliser. Their root system is quite shallow, so always apply mulch on top of the pots.

Blueberries live for a long time in cooler climates (unless you own a puppy) but get heat-stressed in hot, dry summers and consequently have a shorter lifespan.

Liquid-fertilise in late winter, mid spring and mid summer and renew potting mix every three years.

Flowers are borne at the ends of suckers in their second spring. Prune old suckers back to ground level after 3–4 years to encourage new canes.

High-chill varieties

Bluecrop

A tall bush up to 2 metres, with fat juicy berries borne in early December.

Bluerose

A later ripening berry from January through to March. Has heavy crops of large fruit.

Northland

The longest fruiting of the high-chill blueberries, producing from December to March.

Low-chill varieties

Misty

Semi-evergreen bush with lovely autumn colours, producing juicy berries from November to March.

Brightwell

Bears heavy crops from January to March, with pretty pink fruit that ripens to blue.

Sunshine Blue

Masses of small berries ripening in late summer. Prolific bearer.

Sharpe

Lovely flavoured fruit and pretty foliage. Seems to fruit on and off for months. A great partner to Misty.

Such rewarding little plants – I think every garden should have at least four pots of blueberries. The longer you can leave the fruit on the bush, the sweeter the taste. I have to share mine with my dog, Tilly, who has become very nimble at delicately removing them one at a time.

A dog-friendly garden

Being a dog lover, my garden and I have been through a few dogs over the years, and it can be quite a challenge to keep that sweet demeanour when you find half the garden dug up, chewed or both.

Different breeds of dogs will create different kinds of havoc. Some dogs are only interested in digging dirty big craters, some specialise in chewing through the entire retic system with a penchant for pop-up sprinklers, others just love to destroy any new plant you put in the garden yesterday. Puppies prefer to trail everything above ground just to keep you on your toes. Older dogs have the capacity to sit on plants and crush them to death, and dogs like kelpies can jump as high as Spiderman, taking tips on escape tactics from Houdini himself.

The key is to give your dog plenty of mental and physical stimulation. They love chew-toys and spending time playing with you. It's a bit like toddlers – you need to wear them out. Bored puppies and dogs will find their own way of amusing themselves, which you will find most un-amusing when you return home.

The strongest advice I can give is to fence off any part of the garden that is precious or can't take severe pruning with razor-sharp teeth and craters in the vegie patch.

On the topic of fences, sadly there have been some deaths recently from dogs getting into swimming pools and not being able to get out. You need to make sure your dog can't jump over the fence, dig under it or squeeze through any gaps.

Do not rely on dogs having the sense to differentiate between toxic and non-toxic plants. If you have plants that are unsafe for dogs, you must restrict their access until puppies get past the chewing stage or, if your adult dog is a chewer, avoid them in your garden altogether. There are many plants that are on the poisonous list for dogs, and you may be surprised just how many. A few of the most common plants are oleander, brunfelsia, all liliums, wandering jew, many bulbs, stephanotis, hellebore, hydrangea and holly. There is a great book called *Poisonous 2 Pets: Plants poisonous to dogs and cats* by Nicole O'Kane available from the CSIRO. If you think your dog has eaten a poisonous plant, take a piece of it with you to the vet for identification.

It's not just plants that can harm your dog. Any poisons around your home can be a hazard. Rat and mouse bait, snail pellets, herbicides, pesticides, medications and even fertiliser can have a fatal effect on your pet. If you store these in your shed, have them up high as you would with a toddler in the house. There is no such thing as dog-friendly rat and mouse baits. If you suspect your dog or puppy has eaten baits, it's essential to get them to the vet immediately – better to be safe and have them induce vomiting as soon as possible.

If you are planning on getting a puppy and haven't yet finished the garden, I strongly recommend vegies in raised beds with plenty of room between for dogs to walk through. It will save you a lot of heartache and plant replacement. They are puppies and as such do not understand what they have done wrong. It's better to train them by playing with them in other parts of the garden than punish them for something they don't understand. You will also need to find a place where your puppy can go and dig. It will probably proudly show you, so it's better designating one particular spot it's okay to dig than filling in several holes all over the garden. This is really important during the summer months – a dog will find the coolest part of the garden to lie in to escape the heat.

A shady tree and some lawn are vital to keep your dog happy. That gives it somewhere to lie and play and roll. In summer, I fill up one of those shells used for a toddler's sandpit or pool. It's shallow enough for a dog to get in and out easily and deep enough to soak in on really hot days.

Remember, your dog will become part of the family. Its needs are an important factor to consider before you embark (pardon the pun) on adding one to the household.

Pest watch

Watch out for thrips, aphids, webbing caterpillars and scale.

Thrips hang out in large groups. Some are leaf-feeders, others only go for flowers. Their rasping mouthparts cause a mottled silvering appearance on leaves or distorted flowers and fruit. You will find black speckles on the backs of leaves, which is their faeces. For the size of the insect

(1–2 mm long) they seem to poo a lot. There are many natural predators of thrips so if you build up your army of beneficial insects you will rarely have to spray.

Squish aphids sucking the sap out of fresh new growth on plants like roses and lilly pilly (see p. 154).

Webbing caterpillars may be in your melaleucas and callistemons. You can either prune off the affected branches or spray with Dipel or Success.

There are hundreds of different species of scale in Australia feeding on just about all garden plants, including fruit trees. Scale are divided into hard-bodied and soft-bodied and all of them are sap-suckers. Examples of commonly known soft-bodied scale include mealy bug, cottony cushion scale, Chinese wax scale and soft brown scale. Examples of commonly known hard-bodied scale include California red scale, rose scale, San Jose scale, apple scale and white louse scale.

Scale and aphids secrete a liquid called honeydew, which is harvested by ants. In return for the sweet milkshake provided, ants help protect scale from predators and move them around the plant to new feeding grounds.

The *Rodolia cardinalis* ladybird is an absolute champion in controlling cottony cushion scale, and there are many others. The biggest problem with scale is the secondary effect of honeydew on plants – it develops sooty mould. Branches, leaves and fruit can get covered in a black coating which doesn't directly damage plants, but reduces a plant's ability to photosynthesise.

Once you control the scale, there is no honeydew for the sooty mould to grow on. If you have a severe infestation of scale, spray with Eco-Oil or Natrasoap. One week later get the hose and blast them off, which will also get rid of the sooty mould.

All regions

General care

- Oxalis will be appearing throughout the garden. Believe me, if you don't control it as soon as you see it, you will have it as a permanent garden plant. It has lovely soft shamrock leaves and very pretty yellow or violet flowers and is known as wood sorrel and soursob. The root has many tiny bulbils that fall off and grow in every possible space. Forget trying to dig it out – you will spread it further. It's best to heavily mulch it, smother it or sprinkle salt on damp leaves.
- Roses will be making a move and require fertilising to form good flowering buds in spring. A good fertiliser that is high in potassium and has all the other minerals is best for roses – they are hungry feeders at this time of the year.
- Keep tying up climbing plants to control the growth to where you want it.
- Rake up any fallen leaves and scatter around garden beds. Add a light dressing of blood and bone to help break them down to a fabulous soil conditioner.

- Apply lime and blood and bone to the compost heap along with hay and food scraps.

The edible garden

- Citrus gall wasp will start making an impact on citrus trees from this month through to January. Apply Tree Guard 30–50 cm above ground level to the trunk of the tree to form a barrier to prevent insects crawling and codling moth larvae from climbing the tree.
- Fertilise citrus trees after cropping. Apply it to the drip line and freshen up the mulch.
- Time to graft your apple, pear and plum trees onto a two-year-old scion.
- Spray stone fruit trees with a copper-based spray to control peach leaf curl.

Lawn

- Lawns will start to make some new growth so give them the first dressing of fertiliser this month. Check for signs of fungal disease and treat with a lawn fungicide if necessary. They can have a light dressing of compost. Apply a wetting agent along with the fertiliser and water in well.

Pruning

- Give summer-flowering perennials and shrubs a light trim to encourage more compact growth.

- Prune back hibiscus plants by at least a third; remove any diseased wood or crossing branches. The healthy semi-hardwood prunings can be used for cuttings that are 12–15 cm long. After pruning give the plants a dressing of manure and compost. Once new growth emerges you can then fertilise with a high potassium fertiliser.
- Sedum plants will need to have all the old dead stems cut to below ground level to encourage fresh new growth. Apply a liquid fertiliser after cutting back.

Planting and cuttings

- It's a feverish planting time while the weather is still cool and there is still the promise of rain (unless you are up in the tropics). Plant summer-flowering bulbs like the highly perfumed tuberose, Scarborough lily, Amazon lily, hippeastrum and boldly coloured tuberous begonia.
- After frosts have cleared, divide and replant Michaelmas daisy, rudbeckia, lupins and perennial phlox.

Tropical/Subtropical

Edible garden tasks

- Sow Asian greens, asparagus, basil, beetroot, carrot, Chinese cabbage, chives, choko, coriander, cucumber, eggplant, English spinach, French beans, kale, lettuce, mint, okra, parsley, potato, pumpkin, radish, rocket, silverbeet, spring onion, sweet corn, sweet potato, taro, tomato, zucchini.
- Plant out dragon fruit into compost and manure in a sunny position. They will need support as they climb up a trellis.
- Pick custard apples as they ripen and check for mealy bug on the fruit. Spray with Eco-Oil if you have an infestation, but not if there are predators like ladybirds about.
- Feed pawpaw and babaco plants with a fruit tree fertiliser as they flower to get large juicy fruit.
- Strawberries could be in flower now and will need a dressing of sulphate of potash.
- Take 30 cm cuttings of sweet potato plants and lay them horizontally into garden beds with just the top two leaves poking out of the soil. Do not feed too much with manure or high nitrogen fertilisers as you will get lovely leaf growth but not many tubers forming.

- Sow seeds of the New Guinea winged bean (*Psophocarpus tetragonolobus*). They are such fast growers and you can eat every part of the plant. The flowers and leaves are delicious in a salad. The winged beans are best eaten when very young – no longer than 10 cm. The plants only last for about six months but they are worth it.
- Cut back and divide lemongrass plants. Wear gloves as the edges of the leaves are razor-sharp.
- Lift and divide up taro, turmeric and ginger and replant into compost-rich soil. When new shoots appear apply a granular fertiliser.

General garden tasks

- Apply some manure and mulch to ornamental ginger plants, caladiums and turmeric in their late dormancy, just before they emerge again.
- Cut back tree dahlias when they finish flowering. The cuttings can be laid horizontally in the garden to grow new plants.
- Lightly underprune crepe myrtles to show off their beautiful branches. Flowers will form on the new summer growth.
- Repot palms in fresh potting mix, with some manure and straw added to the top layer of the pot.
- Gently pull off the pups that have formed on bromeliads and pot them up separately into individual pots.

- Divide ferns and repot to allow for the new growth in spring. A mixture of cocopeat and potting mix make a good free-draining light soil to grow into.

Temperate/Mediterranean

Edible garden tasks

- Sow artichoke, Asian greens, asparagus, basil, beans, beetroot, carrot, celery, Chinese cabbage, chives, coriander, dill, endive, English spinach, Florence fennel, Jerusalem artichoke, kale, lettuce, mint, onion, parsley, peas, potato, radish, rocket, silverbeet, snake beans, snake gourd, spring onion, tomato, turnip.
- Give root crops and brassicas a drenching of 1 teaspoon of borax to 10 litres of water at seedling stage.
- Layer more hay and manure onto potato plants to get more tubers to form.
- Strawberries could be in flower now and will need a dressing of sulphate of potash. Grow them in tubs to keep them off the ground away from slaters, slugs, snails and bobtail lizards.
- Observe buds on peach and nectarine trees to assess when spraying is needed at bud burst to prevent peach leaf curl. Use a copper-based fungicide.
- Feed deciduous fruiting trees that have reached bud burst stage.

- Thin kiwifruit vines by one-third.
- Plant into the ground choko fruits that have a shoot emerging out of them. Plant the fruit just below ground level and cover with compost and hay. When the vine shoots, add more hay, mounding it up to 15 cm high. Choose a protected position that receives half a day of sun.

General garden tasks

- Cut off the spent flower heads of bulbs as they dry out. This is the time to give your bulbs a feed as they finish flowering and are still green. They will put their energy into next season's flowers.
- Spring-flowering shrubs and trees will be full of buds and now is the time to keep up the water and liquid fertiliser. Make sure the mulch is around the drip line of trees.
- Plant out summer-flowering bulbs such as lilium, November lily, gladioli, hippeastrum, lily-of-the-valley, nerine and Solomon's seal.
- Deadhead sweet peas to encourage more flowers.
- Deadhead camellias that have finished flowering. Apply a liquid fertiliser after pruning.
- Cut back rosemary to keep young shoots developing. Prune back at least a third of the bush.
- Add some beautiful flowering natives into your garden such as Geraldton wax, correa, waratah, boronia, eriostemon and hardenbergia to attract birds and beneficial insects.

- Wattles will be coming into bloom and putting on a dazzling display. Look out for the new hybrid dwarf varieties and only plant wattles that do not pose a weed problem in your area.
- Prune back winter-flowering natives to keep them compact and free-flowering. Fertilise with a native slow-release fertiliser or blood and bone.
- Apply fertiliser to hydrangeas that are developing leaves. You can start applying blueing tonic if you live in alkaline soils and want blue blooms.
- Service the lawn mower and replace blades – mowing commences soon.

Cool/Cold

Edible garden tasks

- Sow artichoke, asparagus, broad beans, broccoli, cabbage, carrot, celery, coriander, endive, English spinach, Jerusalem artichoke, lettuce, mint, onion, peas, potato, radish, rocket, swede, turnip.
- Get some No-Dig potatoes in the ground by growing them under straw. Choose a site that has full sun and is weed-free or has had the weeds whipper-snipped.
- Feed all vegie beds with blood and bone and manure, except in areas where you will be planting out carrots and onions.
- Prune neglected lemon trees to encourage new growth and fruiting wood.

- Prune passionfruit vines now so that the fruit develops and ripens over summer. Always fertilise all the way along the vegetation line after pruning.
- Rake aside mulch in heavy damp areas of the garden – it will allow the soil to dry out and warm up for spring plantings.

General garden tasks

- Bare-rooted roses and ornamental shrubs and trees can still be purchased and planted in August.
- In frost-prone areas it is now safe to prune your roses. Frosts will be over by the time the new shoots come out (see pp. 111–16). Spray with lime sulphur after pruning and remove all leaves from the ground.
- Throw some spring-flowering annuals in garden beds – larkspur, California poppy, carnation, gypsophila, nemesia, sunflower, sweet pea and cosmos.
- This is the best time to get native plants into the ground. Nurseries that specialise in Australian natives will have the biggest selection of species and guide you to the ones that suit your soil type and climate. With native trees, particularly eucalypts, it is better to buy them in tubestock rather than large pots because their root system grows so fast they may become root-bound.

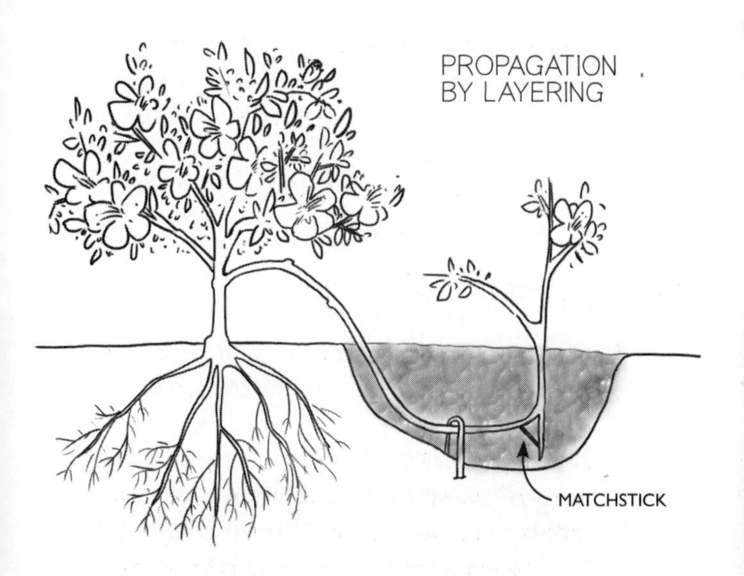

- It's time to propagate azaleas, rhododendrons, viburnum and gardenias by *layering* (see above). Make a cut into the underside of the stem, push a piece of matchstick to keep the cut open, then shallow-bury it in the soil and pin it down with a piece of U-shaped wire.
- Deciduous magnolias can be propagated by air-layering. Make a 10 mm cut into an upward-facing stem just below a node. Wrap the cut with wet sphagnum moss and tie it to the branch using foil or plastic wrap. Tie the top and bottom with tape. You can sever the piece of branch after it develops roots in a couple of months.

September

The benefits of predatory insects

September is the month when many insects emerge after winter and drive gardeners into a frenzy of pest control. All the sap-suckers breed eagerly to feast on fresh new growth and chewing insects devour juicy soft leaves. What gardeners need to be aware of is that in killing insect pests they may also be killing off their natural enemies who would otherwise be doing the work for you. There are many beneficial predatory insects that will keep pest numbers down if you steer clear of pesticides and grow flowering plants that attract them.

In Australia we have around 65,000 described insect species and less than 0.5 per cent are considered to be pests for agriculture and horticulture. Many insects like ladybirds, lacewings and parasitic wasps are beneficial for the home gardener, but all insects play a role in natural cycles – either in decomposing vegetative matter and dead animals or pollinating plants – and all are vital to the earth's ecosystems.

If you decide to create a healthy ecosystem in your own garden you will have to let the insects considered pests build up in number to attract and keep the predatory insects in your area. Your best garden tool should be a magnifying glass so that you can see exactly what's going on in the insect world.

Predatory insects will hang around if they know they have a consistent food source. They need a place to lay the next generation, which is usually where the host is feeding on your plants. It's wonderful to know that buying beneficial insects has now become much easier, making organic gardening methods more accessible for those who wish to grow their own food without the use of pesticides.

Many of the predatory wasps, green lacewings and the pollen beetle need a feed of nectar before they lay eggs, so incorporating flowers within the garden is another way of attracting insects. Broad-spectrum insecticides will kill these little helpers, so it's important for gardeners to observe first and then consider whether they need any control measures at all.

Remember that some pesticides have a flow-on effect up the food chain. We are at the top of the food chain, so ultimately all the pesticides and herbicides used to grow crops that feed the animals that we eat are going to end up in us.

Lawns

In the past ten years lawn has copped a real flogging as the bad guy in a sustainable world. It's time to set the record straight because there is so much misinformation regarding the negative impact lawn has on the environment.

New varieties of warm-season turf are very drought-tolerant and, if planted out correctly with the right preparation, they use little more water than a native garden.

The key here is the proper preparation to the soil before laying.

Water-efficient lawns like Sir Walter Buffalo, Palmetto, Sapphire, Empire Zoysia, Kenda and Village Green are an asset to sustainable urban spaces, not a drawback.

We don't need vast amounts of lawn around our houses, but we certainly need some to offset the urban heat island effect created by hard surfaces and the lack of open spaces. Green spaces entice us outdoors to live a healthier and less stressful lifestyle.

Turf is ten times better at reducing nutrient, sediment and chemical pollution than any other crop, and hundreds of times better than hard surfaces like paving and concrete.

It is well documented that some lawn and shade trees around the house will cool the surroundings down by as much as 10 degrees, and more than this, they'll provide a habitat for a whole ecosystem. The cooling effect of 100 sqm of lawn is as much as running four air-conditioners.

Artificial turf, on the other hand, absorbs heat and becomes far too hot to even stand on (apart from the fact it's difficult to clean dog and cat urine and faeces off). Not the place to let toddlers and babies crawl over. Ultimately, it goes into landfill.

Most turf farms will supply products to help to establish new turf. Compost, loam, fertiliser, wetting agent and water retention products are a must if you want a trouble-free lawn that requires little watering and fertilising over future years. Do not scrimp on this side of things. If you can't afford to do the appropriate preparation, don't get the lawn until you can. If you are getting a contractor to lay your turf, ask them exactly what prep they do and what products they use.

And while on my soapbox, don't buy cheap types of turf. Couch would have to be the most invasive weed on the planet. It may only cost you $4 a metre to buy, but it's going to cost you $30 a metre to try to get it out of your garden beds for the next ten years.

So fellas, on the subject of fertilising, you only need one handful per square metre and only four times a year. Established lawn doesn't need phosphorus at all so look at what your fertiliser says on the bag. I don't know why blokes love lawns but it's a fact they do. It's their kingdom and their pride. Blokes also love pouring on eight times as much fertiliser as needed. Their reasoning is that if 1 kg is good for the lawn, 4 kg must be better. Wrong. Most of that fertiliser will run off into our waterways and grow algal bloom. Not only that, you will have to mow the lawn three times as much.

Did You Know?

Turf is highly efficient at taking carbon from the air, locking it up in the soil in its extensive root system and releasing oxygen back into the atmosphere. One hectare of turf can lock up 3 tonnes of carbon for thirty years.

Varieties

There are pros and cons to each lawn variety and it's important to do your homework and select the right lawn for your lifestyle. Turf farms have great websites that offer information on keeping your lawn healthy.

Sir Walter Buffalo

I have to say it's my favourite lawn. I have large dogs and a family that hammers my back lawn and it's been trouble-free and looking great for ten years now.

Sir Walter turf is a soft-leaf buffalo with deep roots, a low thatch habit and a tight growth sward. It stays greener throughout summer and winter and is disease-resistant.

Another benefit is that it has proven shade tolerance so this makes it ideal for small courtyard areas and under trees.

This buffalo is not invasive and responds to a harsh mowing every few years.

Palmetto

A soft-leaf buffalo variety with great shade tolerance. Like Sir Walter, it is drought-tolerant and maintains its deep green colour throughout the year. A good lawn for kids and dogs alike and outruns any weed competition.

Sapphire

A very soft-leaf buffalo that is finer than other soft-leaf buffalos when it is mature. It's also one of the more frost-tolerant lawns, coping with –10 degrees in winter, so it's a good one for colder climates. It is a deep blue-green colour, grows well in dappled shade, is drought-tolerant and outcompetes weeds.

Queensland Blue

A soft-leaf lawn (*Digitaria didactyla*) with a very soft dense grass and a beautiful blue-green colour. It needs full sun and does well in coastal areas with high humidity, but doesn't thatch up like couch. It is slower growing and less invasive then couch but not as drought-tolerant as the buffalo types.

Kenda and Village Green

This is *Pennisetum clandestinum*, which is a sterile form of kikuyu that does not produce viable seed, eliminating the problems of seed dispersal into native bushland. Both types manage to survive the winter better and produce a dense rhizome growth, making them more drought-tolerant. Good for dogs and kids, these lawns will need full sun and are practically indestructible, surviving neglect and extreme heat.

Empire Zoysia

You may know Zoysia by the name of Empire or Empress Grass. A fantastic drought-tolerant lawn, it has a soft-leaf shaft, making it great for children. The downside is that it has a slower growth rate than other lawns, and takes a long time to recover if you have a few kids and dogs. The upside is that it requires much less frequent mowing.

Pest watch

Snails and slugs can be controlled with copper tape, Slugit, Escar-Go, iron-based Multiguard slug and snail pellets and your size-8 boot.

Aphids will be sucking the sap out of fresh new growth on just about every plant in the garden. You can use the squish between two fingers method or spray with an oil or pyrethrum if there are no natural predators doing the work for you. Ladybirds, wasps and lacewings are fabulous predators on aphids.

Webbing caterpillars will still be around attacking native plants. You can either prune off the affected branches or spray with Dipel or Success.

All regions

General care

- It's feeding time – the whole garden will be needing some extra nutrients as it comes out of its winter sleep. Use a good quality fertiliser that has all the micronutrients. Feed the soil with compost and seaweed solution to build up potassium levels and feed microbes in the soil.
- Deciduous magnolias, viburnum, weigela and philadelphus will be coming into bloom. Feed them when they finish flowering with a granular slow-release fertiliser.

- Liquid-fertilise all vegetables and annual flowering plants. Give a dressing of blood and bone or native fertiliser to Australian native plants. Always water in after fertilising.
- Perennials that die down in the winter will be emerging from the soil. Use a seaweed solution with a liquid fertiliser to help them develop flowering stems.
- Repot and rejuvenate indoor plants with new potting mix. Drench them with half-strength seaweed solution to encourage new root growth.
- Give orchids a feed of liquid fertiliser at half the normal strength.
- Daphne plants will appreciate a drench of Epsom salts – dissolve 1 tablespoon in a 9 litre watering can.
- Apply blueing tonic to your hydrangeas – pour the liquid at the base of the plant and apply every four weeks until flower buds form.
- Tie epiphytic orchids and bromeliads into the southern side of trees to add interest to tree trunks.

Pruning

- Once the threat of frosts is over it is safe to prune back growth that has been frost-burnt. Take it back to the fresh green growth or to new green buds that are emerging off the stems.

- You can prune hedges back hard to get stronger and more dense growth before the summer months.
- Prune back banksias that have finished flowering. Only go as far back as the semi-hardwood; do not cut back into the old wood as the entire branch will die back.

Planting

- Get flowering plants into the vegie patch to attract beneficial insects. Any flower that has pollen will be good for native bees and predatory wasps. Native plants and any of the daisy type flowers will attract insects.
- Plant out dahlia tubers, nerine, lycoris and pineapple lily.
- Divide chrysanthemum, agapanthus, mondo grass, lamb's ear, gazania and clivia plants. Cut off diseased leaves and replant into freshly composted soil. Add a dressing of manure and slow-release fertiliser.
- Fill bare gaps in the garden with brightly coloured foliage plants such as cordyline, coleus, aglaonema, croton and phormium into dappled light or shady spots.

Tropical/Subtropical

Edible garden tasks

- Sow Asian greens, asparagus, basil, capsicum, carrot, chilli, Chinese cabbage, chives, choko, coriander, cucumber, eggplant, English spinach, French beans, lettuce, melon, mint, parsley, pumpkin, radish, rocket, rosella, silverbeet, snake beans, spring onion, sweet corn, sweet potato, tomato, zucchini.
- Get the sweet corn plots going. They are better planted in blocks of at least ten plants for wind pollination to be effective.
- Scatter coriander and basil seeds around the garden – they like being self-sown and hate root disturbance.
- As the weather warms up, select tomatoes that will cope with the wet season heat. Cherry tomatoes will still give you fruit when temperatures soar.
- Get taro plants into the ground – they will grow rapidly over the wet season.
- Replenish soil in vegie beds. Make sure there is plenty of drainage before the wet season sets in. Check for the presence of termites.
- See if pumpkins are ready for harvest by checking the tendril that goes from the stem to the base of the pumpkin – it should be dry and fissured. Tap the melon: if it sounds hollow it's right to pick. Always retain 10 cm of the stem.

- Avocado trees will need watering regularly now. The mulch should be 10 cm thick, but nowhere near the trunk.
- Banana plants will need flooding and feeding with a complete fertiliser. Once the hands of bananas have formed and they are a good size you can cut off the flower. Cook it up in a stir-fry, it's delicious. (See more on pp. 27–9.)
- Star fruit trees will have many flowers and fruit developing so will need extra watering and a feed. They respond well to liquid fertiliser and trace elements applied as a foliar feed.
- Prune lanky pawpaw trees, cut 5 cm above a leaf scar and put a plastic laundry bucket on top for six months to stop it from rotting.
- Prune Barbados cherry plants (*Malpighia emarginata*) to keep them from becoming straggly and weak.
- Passionfruit vines can be given a prune to control the rampant growth that will come when the wet season starts.

General garden tasks

- Keep birdbaths and ponds topped up during the dry season. The birds and lizards will come to visit and help with pest control.
- Take cuttings of frangipanis before the wet season. Allow them to callous over for a couple of weeks before potting up into potting mix.

- The drumstick tree (*Moringa oleifera*) can be grown from cuttings 20 cm long. Every part of this tree can be eaten and it is an important food plant in India.
- Prune hibiscus plants by cutting out any diseased wood and crossing branches. Cut back all other growth by a third. All the prunings can be used as cuttings for new plants to give to friends.
- Pull up the entire desert rose plant out of the soil to expose the root system. Replant it at a much shallower level, leaving the top parts of the roots exposed. This will help form a bigger bulbous bottom.
- Get an impervious cover on the ground to prevent weeds taking hold over the wet season. Old carpet is perfect; don't use cardboard as it will attract termites.
- Clean up all garden rubbish before the cyclone season. Garden rubbish can also attract snakes trying to keep cool in the warmer months – another reason to remove it.

Temperate/Mediterranean

Edible garden tasks

- Sow artichoke, Asian greens, asparagus, basil, beans, beetroot, carrot, celery, Chinese cabbage, chives, coriander, dill, eggplant, Florence fennel, Jerusalem artichoke, kale, leek, lettuce, melon, mint, onion, parsley, peas, potato, radish, rocket, silverbeet, snake gourd, spring onion, sweet corn, tomato, turnip, zucchini.
- Revamp the vegie patch, changing from winter to summer crops. Add some new compost, manure and re-mulch. Check to make sure the soil is still holding moisture – use a wetting agent if the soil seems dry.
- Sow seeds of annuals in your vegie bed to attract beneficial insects. Most of the edible plants we grow need an insect pollinator so it's wise to put flowers among your vegies.
- Sow carrot and parsnip seeds directly into the ground. Make sure the area is weed-free.
- As potatoes grow, mound up the leaves with compost, hay and a small amount of blood and bone.
- Mulch strawberry plants with pea hay or lupin mulch, liquid-feed with a high-potassium fertiliser. If slaters are eating your fruit, use diatomaceous earth around the edge of the pot or underneath the leaves; do *not* use it on the flowers as bees that pick it up when they collect pollen will die.

- Give all fruit trees and vegies a dressing of sulphate of potash to develop flowers and fruit. Trace elements can also be dissolved in water and used as a foliar feed to fruit trees to address problems with mineral deficiencies.
- Apply a citrus fertiliser with trace elements to all citrus for the spring flush of growth. Water in well.
- It's also a great time to plant out citrus trees. The soil is warming up but the weather is mild enough for active growth.
- Crabapples will be in full bloom now with the promise of tiny apples that make excellent jam. Make sure they are mulched and keep the water up to them until fruiting has finished – then you can prune the trees.
- Prune back passionfruit vines to promote summer fruiting. Apply a complete fertiliser the length of the vine.
- Spray grapevines with lime sulphur at bud burst and apply a fertiliser along the root zone.

General garden tasks

- Get some organic-based liquid fertiliser on the entire garden as it wakes up from its winter slumber.
- Hardy waterlilies are re-emerging now and you will need to apply new aquatic slow-release fertiliser tablets. Top up pots with an aquatic planting mix (see p. 15).

- Apply sulphate of aluminium or blueing tonic monthly to hydrangeas until November to ensure blue flowers.
- Visit your local nursery to see the new native plants for this year. Plant breeders are developing some amazing new varieties of native plants that perform better in our gardens and are more suitable for the smaller block sizes.
- Newly planted natives will need to be cared for when the rains stop. Make sure you have them all mulched and don't let them dry out as their root systems will still be small.
- Prune back callistemons that have become straggly or where all the growth is just at the top. You can prune them back by 50 per cent.

Cool/Cold

Edible garden tasks

- Sow artichoke, asparagus, beetroot, broccoli, cabbage, carrot, celery, coriander, dill, endive, English spinach, Florence fennel, Jerusalem artichoke, kohlrabi, lettuce, mint, onion, parsley, parsnip, silverbeet, snow peas, spring onion, potato, radicchio, radish, rocket, swede, turnip.
- Get stuck into the bare vegie beds. Dig in some manure to feed the worms and microbes, add dolomite lime, compost and hay. Let it all settle for a couple of weeks before planting out.

- Start your tomato plants off in a protected position and plant out when there is no danger of frost. Liquid-feed them once you plant them into the garden. (See more on pp. 165–6.)
- Get those peas in – it's the perfect time. Remember to dig in 1 handful of dolomite lime per square metre before planting the seed.
- Plant out rhubarb crowns into improved soil. They will need summer watering but make good growth from this month on.
- Plant out leafy greens and herbs to make the most of the warmer weather.
- Spike around trees to break up any compaction and spread compost and manure around the base.
- Squish any woolly aphids that may be settling on apple trees. If you leave it too long you will have a plague.
- Tip-prune gooseberry bushes, checking for signs of mildew. Leaving the bush more open so that air flows through the centre of the bush helps to alleviate this problem.

General garden tasks

- Finish pruning hydrangea, ceanothus and buddleia. Liquid-fertilise after pruning.
- Sow seeds of ageratum, cosmos, cornflower, nigella, poppy, nemesia, rudbeckia and geum for a colourful display through spring and early summer.

- Plant out summer-flowering bulbs such as Solomon's seal, galtonia, zephyranthes, iris and lily-of-the-valley.
- Allow cyclamen plants to dry out now that the foliage has died down. You can leave them in the pot tipped on its side to prevent moisture from getting in and repot when they shoot again in January.
- Repot any house plant that is root-bound into fresh potting mix. Give all house plants a liquid feed to encourage spring growth.
- Build up the mulch at the base of clematis vines to protect them from the warmer weather. Tie tendrils to help support the flowers.
- Give lawns a feed with a slow-release fertiliser that has little or no phosphorus. You can make up your own by mixing blood and bone with 10 per cent potash and 5 per cent rock dust. Keep the blades high on the mower until the days are a bit warmer.
- Visit open gardens, garden festivals and botanical parks to see the wonderful displays of spring-flowering natives and bulbs.

October

Tomatoes

People start wanting to plant out tomatoes in August, but unless you live in a tropical area, this is not a good time. The soil needs to be warm and the daylight hours longer, so wait until October. Having spent many months enduring rock-hard, completely tasteless tomatoes, we are all keen to get some flavour back into the mix. I truly believe nothing beats the taste of outdoor grown tomatoes that are sun-ripened.

I'm a big fan of growing from open pollinated seed because the range of tomatoes available is astonishing. We are now seeing more of the heirloom range of tomatoes hitting the seedlings stands, so the choice is improving. If you check out the Diggers Club and Eden Seeds you will find they supply up to fifty different varieties of heirloom tomato and have trialled hundreds.

In 1993 Heronswood conducted a taste test on thirty different tomatoes with chefs, seed merchants and garden experts. The winner was Tommy Toe ranking 72.81 out of 100, and the worst were the supermarket tomatoes at 44.44. If you are looking for a big blousy slicing tomato go for the Costoluto Genovese, Mortgage Lifter, Grosse Lisse and Black Krim.

There's even a tomato you can hurl at football referees, politicians and people knocking at your door to flog you stuff you don't want and didn't ask for – it's aptly named Granny's Throwing Tomato. It's a very popular Italian tomato that I believe has coloured Silvio Berlusconi's jacket in recent years. Clive Blazey from Diggers has described it as 'curving in the air like a Warney wrong 'un. Productive, early and subversive.' You've got to love that.

The trick to getting them to flower and fruit early is to treat them mean in the first three weeks of growth. Allow them to wilt before watering. There's no truth to the advice of lateral pruning to increase yield, in fact it decreases yield. The only pruning needed is to take off the lower branches so water splashing from the ground to the stems doesn't carry disease up the plant.

Always allow ample spacings between bushes to allow airflow and sunlight into the foliage. Good quality compost, old manure and blood and bone with a bit of sulphate of potash will grow healthy plants. Liquid-fertilise once flowers develop over the bush and stake them BEFORE they fall over onto the ground.

Strawberries

Strawberries are grown all year round, but plants usually become available in nurseries in the warmer months from October through to May. In tropical climates the season is shorter and it's best to plant in autumn.

It's so exciting to go out into the garden in the morning and pluck fresh little red jewels off a plant and straight into your mouth – taste explosion.

Strawberries are so easy to grow. Basically, if you can fill a pot up with potting mix, you can grow strawberries. The flower is beautiful, the plant is deep-green and lush and the fruit is sensational. They are an excellent source of vitamin C and folic acid. There are hundreds of strawberry varieties today that have all been bred from the few original wild species.

Unfortunately, birds, slaters, snails, rats, dogs and lizards all love them as much as we do. The best way of avoiding trouble from these competitors is to grow your strawberry plants in a container up off the ground. Slaters and snails are usually the main problem and are easily dealt with if you put a copper barrier around the container.

Strawberries need free-draining soil that is slightly acidic (pH 6.0–6.5) with added compost, cow poo and mulch. Chicken poo tends to be too alkaline for strawberries so use it sparingly.

They like sun, but need protecting from the hot afternoon sun in the summer months. The great advantage of growing strawberries in a container is that you can move them around to just morning sun in summer and all-day sun in the winter months.

Strawberry plants need to be watered every day when they start to fruit, so growing them in a container makes this easy and prevents water wastage. They also need regular feeding when the flowers appear. If you grow them in a container, reduce the fertilising to half-strength to avoid overfeeding. You can use a good quality biodynamic liquid fertiliser with added humates once every three weeks once flowering commences.

Growing strawberry plants from runners

Don't make the mistake of ripping a runner off from the parent plant, stuffing it into the ground and expecting it to grow. Nine times out of ten it will die. Here is what you will need to do:

1. Cut off a strong runner that looks disease-free.
2. Dig a wide hole and make a little pile of dirt in the centre, a bit like building a volcano in a hole.
3. Put the runner on top of the volcano and fill in the hole, making sure the crown of the plant is above the soil.
4. Water in well and mulch around it with straw.

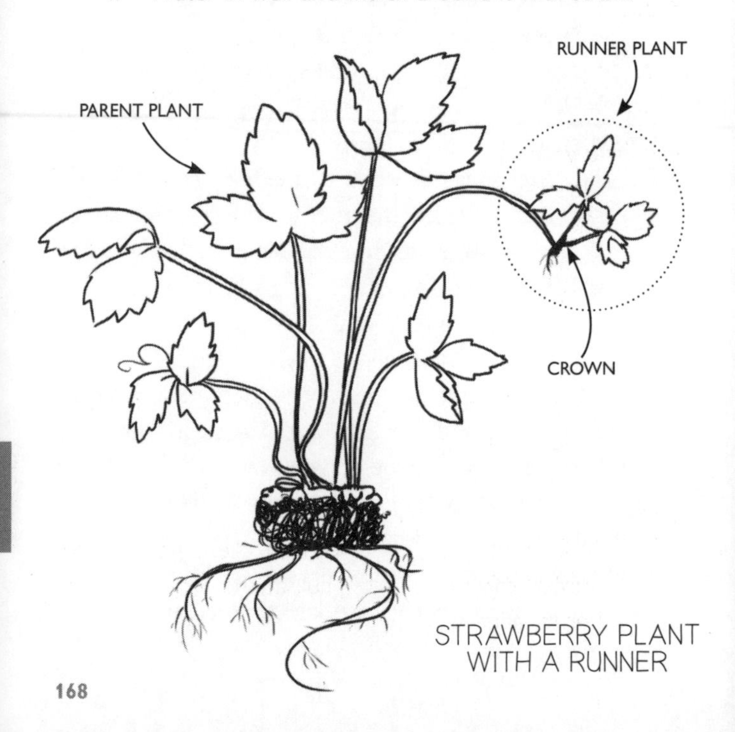

STRAWBERRY PLANT WITH A RUNNER

Diseases

A common fungal disease is botrytis (grey mould), which looks like a fuzzy grey or off-white growth on the fruit. The leaves can show wilting, yellowing and circular black spots. You'll need to remove and bin the affected parts. Prevention is better than cure in the case of botrytis. Avoid overhead watering as the fungal spores travel by water splash and are also airborne. Try not to overcrowd the plants – allow lots of air circulation.

Varieties

Adina

Great taste, fragrance and appearance. The large, bright-red fruit is low-acid and sweet.

Fragaria vesca

The wild strawberry (or European woodland strawberry) will make a beautiful addition to your garden. It will also grow well in hanging baskets. The fruit is tiny but mighty, with the most intense taste and fragrance.

Hokowase

A Japanese variety with wedge-shaped fruit that's soft, sweet and acid-free.

Kiewa

A very fragrant strawberry with excellent flavour and an upturned calyx (the green hull at the top). Available October to January.

Lowanna

The fruits are conical-shaped, large and bright red. Available October to June.

Millewa

A very large, conical-shaped fruit, that fruits heavily twice a year – in spring to early summer, and again in autumn to early winter.

Red Gauntlet

This popular commercial variety produces a large crop over a long period. The fruit is light red and medium sized. A great strawberry for the hotter climates.

Rubygem

A Queensland variety with short, conical, dark red fruit. It has great flavour and medium acidity and fruits earlier than most varieties.

Sweetest

This variety has been bred for sweetness. The medium-sized fruit grows on a compact bush, making it ideal for container growing.

Sweetie

Sweetie has lovely pink flowers rather than white. It has good flavour and fruits abundantly over a long period.

Tallara

A very prolific variety with large, deep-red fruit.

Tioga

Tioga produces large, firm fruit from spring right through to late autumn.

Torrey

This Californian variety is great for the hotter climates. The plants are strong upright growers with large leaves and fruit to match. An early fruiter in spring and early summer – a short season, but it bears heavily when it fruits.

Strawberries have so many uses, but my favourite is to soak them in Cointreau and plop them into champagne – good health being foremost on my mind.

Pest watch

Azalea lacebug attacks more than just azaleas. They cling to the underside of leaves of rhododendrons, viburnums, flowering quince, crabapple and cotoneaster. Spray with a botanical oil like Eco-Oil, a soap spray like Natrasoap, or Beat-a-Bug.

Aphids will still be attacking new growth on plants (see p. 154) and the white cedar moth (known as cape lilac moth in the West) will be chewing on the foliage of these trees. They come in their thousands and will invade your house, shed and even climb up curtains. The hairy caterpillars climb up the tree at night to feed on the foliage then descend at dawn, either by a long silken thread or crawling down the trunk. The caterpillars are active during the warmer months. They may come as early as September, with more generations hatching right through to December. Control measures include banding and spraying. For banding, tie a length of hessian or shadecloth 1 metre wide around the trunk of the tree from ground level. Sprinkle tomato and vegetable dust or derris dust around the top of the hessian. Always wear a mask and gloves when using dusts. You will need to top it up every 4–5 days. Never use these dusts around ponds – they are deadly to fish and frogs.

You can spray clusters of caterpillars either at dawn or dusk with Dipel or Success or pyrethrum. Add a few drops of dishwashing detergent so that the pyrethrum penetrates through the body hairs of the caterpillar. Make sure you spray the butt of the trees, along fence lines and anywhere the caterpillars could harbour in the daytime.

Fruit fly

Fruit fly is a major problem for every state in Australia and the home gardener has a responsibility to help control both the Queensland fruit fly (Qfly), *Bactrocera tryoni*, and the Mediterranean fruit fly (Medfly), *Ceratitis capitata*.

If you grow fruit you will need to prepare for fruit fly attack. Their populations build up all spring and summer until the cooler weather hits and they will overwinter to watch the football. There are a number of strategies you will need to put into place:

- **Hygiene:** the most important factor in fruit fly control. Never let infected fruit lie on the ground, and pick and treat any fruit that has been stung. You can put infected fruit in a black plastic bag, tie a knot at the top and leave it in the sun for 7 days, or put the fruit in a bucket with water and a splash of kerosene for 5 days. Medfly will survive in water for many days so the kerosene is necessary to cut off their supply of oxygen. If you use the plastic bag method you can later feed this to the chooks or livestock, but keep the bag away from crows, rats, dogs and other hungry pests.
- **Pruning:** prune your tree to a manageable size where you can easily spray, bait and pick the fruit. If the fruit is too high up in the tree you will be less likely to spray effectively or pick ripening fruit.
- **Chooks and bantams:** many people incorporate their fruit trees into the chook enclosure. Chooks will scratch up and eat emerging adults, larvae and pupae, and any fallen fruit. Fearless and vigilant, these little home-helpers will also reward you with eggs.
- **Exclusion bags:** these are individual bags you tie around the fruit that give total protection from fruit fly. They are available in different sizes and some are more like a sleeve that fits horizontally off the branch. They are also used on crops such as tomato, capsicum and eggplant. You should use trapping (p. 174) and splash baits (p. 176) in combination with exclusion bags to reduce fruit fly populations.

- **Trapping:** traps are more effective if they are hung in trees all year round to diminish adult populations. They attract the adults using pheromones, aromatic food or visual means. Pheromone traps contain a male or female hormone which attracts the adult, and insecticide inside the trap, which kills the fly. Wet or food traps contain a liquid that has a source of protein attractive to both sexes. The pH of the liquid food appears to be an important factor, as they seem to prefer an alkaline level. A relatively new trap has entered the market called CeraTrap – a bait specifically for capturing Medfly but which is also effective against Qfly, especially females. It is made up of hydrolysed proteins and has been highly successful. If you have a chook pen, you will need to put CeraTrap around it as fruit fly will be attracted to the proteins in chicken manure. Place the traps 5 metres apart at 1.5–2 metres above the ground in a shady part of the tree – this will capture any adults in the area.
- **Homemade traps:** traps need to have several entry holes at the top of a container (such as a plastic bottle) and at least 3 cm of liquid (see recipes). You will also need a cap or cover that protects the trap from rain. You could put two traps in each tree and one in a non-fruiting tree to lure them away from your fruit trees. The entry holes should have a diameter of 8 mm for Medfly and 10 mm for Qfly.

Trap Recipes

Many people have their own favourite recipes, some containing horse urine, but for the less adventurous try these ones. Your kitchen cupboard seems a lot less risky than running down a horse.

Traps will need to be cleaned and refilled every few weeks. Remember, during hot weather the liquid will evaporate and may need filling more often.

Qfly traps

- 1 litre water
- 1 cup sugar
- 1 tablespoon dry yeast
- 1 tablespoon vegemite

Mix all ingredients and place in a jar for 4 days before using.

Medfly traps

- 600 ml water
- Juice of 3 oranges
- 25 grams baking powder
- 1 gram potassium carbonate (potash)

Mix all ingredients and dilute 1:10 with water.

- **Foliage splash baits:** these are sprays that contain a food attractant (protein) and an insecticide such as spinosad (derived from soil bacteria and classified as organic). The female fruit fly needs the protein in order to mature her eggs, but both male and female adult Qfly and Medfly are attracted to the bait. The bait is applied as a thick spray aimed at the middle of the tree on the trunk, stems and centre foliage. Splash baiting should start as soon as you have fruit fly caught in traps, or at least 7 weeks before fruit ripens, or when fruit reaches half-size. Apply the bait in the morning when fruit fly are at their most active. After gorging on the bait, the insecticide kills them. Try not to get bait onto the fruit. In high-risk areas you can apply the bait to non-fruiting trees. You will need to reapply the bait after rain.
- **Cover spraying:** this treatment involves an insecticide spray that completely covers all parts of the tree to kill fruit fly at various stages of its life cycle, from egg to adult. However, this will not prevent the female from stinging the fruit. At the time of printing there was no registered organic cover spray. Organic alternatives to cover spraying include Eco-Naturalure, Nature's Way Fruit Fly Control, CeraTrap and Wild May Fruit Fly Attractant.

The bottom line is that no single control measure will protect your trees from fruit fly. You will need to use a combination of traps, splash baits and exclusion bags if you wish to protect your fruit organically. Personally I think it's well worth it.

All regions

General care

- Apply mulch to all garden beds.
- Feed up spring-flowering bulbs for the next year's flowers.
- Start up the spring compost heap. Have a bale of hay nearby to help keep the carbon levels high. Cover the heap with old carpet or hessian to keep the heat in. (See more on pp. 25–7.)
- Check your gutters for leaf build-up to ensure maximum flow from spring rains enters your rainwater tanks.
- Check the whole reticulation system to make sure there are no blockages in sprinklers or drippers and that flush valves are working. Work through station by station. This includes any greywater systems that service garden beds.
- Start your fruit fly control measures (see pp. 172–7). Either wrap fruit in exclusion bags or sleeves or fully insect-net the tree after flowering. Hang baits from trees and spray with Naturalure or spinosad. Refresh baits regularly.

- Remove any suckers that are growing from the base of trees – they will detract from the shape of the tree and may eventually take over. This is particularly important for any grafted trees, including eucalypts. The rootstock is often more robust than the scion.
- Fertilise gardenias and azaleas with 1 tablespoon of iron chelates and 2 teaspoons of Epsom salts in a 9 litre watering can and pour it over the leaf tissue and into the soil.

The edible garden

- Protect vegetable seedlings by placing beer traps nearby. Check early morning and late evening to collect and squash.
- You will need to tie up the stems of tomato bushes every fortnight as they grow.

Pruning

- Clean up gymea lilies, cut off all the lower leaves and prune the flowering stem down to the base.
- Prune non-repeat spring-flowering roses after flowering has finished. Apply a rose fertiliser and a dressing of compost and manure to boost summer growth.
- If you haven't already done so, prune back clumps of kangaroo paw down to 10 cm, including the flowering stems. This helps to control ink-spot disease and develop new flowering stems.

Planting

- Look at any bare patches in the garden and decide if they need to be filled with new plants or if 'less is more'. Sometimes if we overcrowd plants we miss the majesty of individual species. Negative spaces also allow us to put in sculptures, birdbaths or interesting elements that are not plant-based.
- This is the best time of the year for hanging baskets. Refresh with new soil, water retention crystals and slow-release fertiliser. Fill them with succulents, summer-flowering annuals or plants that will cascade over the edge.
- Plant out summer-flowering annuals such as cosmos, zinnia, portulaca, petunia, salvia and nigella.
- Plant summer-flowering bulbs such as gladiolus, nerine, gloriosa, windflowers, autumn crocus and dahlia tubers.
- Divide and replant clivia that may need thinning out to improve their flowering.

Tropical/Subtropical

Edible garden tasks

- Sow Asian greens, basil, capsicum, carrot, chilli, chives, choko, coriander, cucumber, eggplant, Florence fennel, French beans, ginger, lettuce, melon, okra, parsley, pumpkin, rosella, snake beans, spring onion, squash, sweet corn, sweet potato, tomato, zucchini.
- Foliar-feed all tropical fruit trees, including bananas, once every three weeks. Apply liquid potash to encourage better fruiting and thicken up cell walls.
- Ensure bananas have only three main stems – one leader that will fruit this summer and two suckers to replace the main stem after it fruits. Feed banana plants with chicken manure and water deeply twice a week. They need lots of feeding and water at this time of the year. You will not get proper bunches forming if they are starved. (See more on pp. 27–9.)
- Prop up mango branches that are weighed down with the fruit. Use forked sticks. If you have problems with fruit bats and possums put a protective bag around the fruit, and a plastic sleeve at the base of the tree to prevent possums from climbing up the trunk.
- Stop overhead watering cucumber, pumpkin, watermelon, rockmelon, zucchini and squash. The

warmer, more humid weather is going to cause powdery mildew to flourish on all the cucurbit plants. It's best to water at ground level to keep the leaves dry.

- Plant out some local bush tucker plants. They will establish a good root system during the wet season. Put in with compost and a native slow-release fertiliser. Water until the rains start.
- Harvest sweet potatoes and clear the beds every 6 months to get pest-free tubers. Tubers left in the ground too long will be eaten out by potato weevil.
- Ginger and turmeric will start shooting now. Wait until the shoots are 15 cm long before building up the soil around them with compost and mulch.
- Root crops like taro, cassava and yam can be planted now the weather and soil are warming up.
- Cut back lemongrass and use the prunings as mulch. Wear good gloves so the edges of the leaves don't rip your skin to shreds.
- Bring a pot of basil and mint to sit on the kitchen bench for cooking.

General garden tasks

- Apply a 50/50 mix of chicken manure and straw to bamboo clumps to encourage growth. Water deeply and step back to watch it bolt.

- Prune back allamanda plants by 50 per cent to encourage new growth that holds the flowers. Always feed after pruning tropical plants.
- Agapanthus will have fat flowering buds and will need fertilising with a potassium-based fertiliser.

Temperate/Mediterranean

Edible garden tasks

- Sow Asian greens, basil, beetroot, broccoli, capsicum, carrot, chilli, chives, coriander, cucumber, eggplant, Florence fennel, French beans, leek, lettuce, melon, okra, onion, parsley, potato, pumpkin, radicchio, rocket, spring onion, squash, strawberry, swede, sweet corn, sweet potato, tomato, zucchini.
- Plant sweet corn seeds every four weeks to have a continuous supply over summer.
- Plant strawberries in containers or hanging pots (see pp. 166–71). Liquid-fertilise strawberry plants in areas with highly alkaline soil and apply pine needle mulch.
- Thin out deciduous fruit trees to produce larger, better-quality fruit.
- As potatoes grow, mound up the leaves with compost, hay and a small amount of blood and bone.
- Lift and divide rhubarb plants. Replant into free-draining soil that had manure and compost added three weeks before.

General garden tasks

- Now the soil is warming up you can plant out hibiscus, citrus, bougainvillea and Rangoon creeper.
- Cut back red fountain grass to ground level and divide clumps.
- Prune back hedges to create fresh new growing tips. Try to have the base of the hedge slightly wider than the top so that sunlight enters the whole plant. This prevents dieback on growth that receives no sunlight.
- Start liquid-fertilising indoor plants. Add a little sulphate of potash to the base of pots and water in well.
- Divide cymbidium orchids if they have filled the pot. Carefully separate the sets and replant into an orchid mix, not soil-based potting mix. It needs to be very free-draining. Add orchid slow-release fertiliser and water until you see the water running from the base of the pot.
- Apply a slow-release fertiliser to native climbers such as hardenbergia, pandorea, billardiera and sollya.
- Give a light tip-prune to native plants that will flower in December.
- Boronia, Geraldton wax, grevillea, prostanthera and callistemon will have finished flowering and can be pruned back by a third. Geraldton wax can be cut back by two-thirds. Fertilise with a native slow-release fertiliser and water in well.

- Camellias and azaleas that have finished flowering can be fertilised with a granular fertiliser.
- Lovely hoverflies will be coming through the garden in swarms as they catch the winds that bring them from up north. They are great predators for aphids, thrips and scale as they lay their eggs among these insects for an easy feed.
- Plant out dahlia tubers into a sunny spot in improved soil. Don't be too heavy-handed with manure as this will cause the tubers to rot. Keep straw mulch away from the stems as they are susceptible to powdery mildew.

Cool/Cold

Edible garden tasks

- Sow artichoke, Asian greens, broccoli, carrots, cauliflower, chives, coriander, cucumber, dill, eggplant, endive, English spinach, Florence fennel, French beans, kale, kohlrabi, leek, lettuce, onion, parsley, parsnip, peas, potato, pumpkin, radicchio, rocket, spring onion, squash, strawberry, swede, sweet corn, tomato, zucchini.
- Plant strawberries in containers or hanging pots (see pp. 166–71).
- Plant a patch of potatoes into improved soil. As they grow keep mounding up the leaves with compost, hay and a small amount of blood and bone.

- Plant out all the warm-weather vegies and get them growing quickly by applying a liquid feed at seedling stage.
- Plant out pumpkin seeds directly in the ground in a sunny spot. Give them lots of space to run. The first flowers are usually male. Female flowers form later on side shoots, so once the runners are 2 metres long, cut 10 cm off the ends to encourage more side shoots. If there aren't many bees around, pull the male flower off and tickle the inside of the female flower. Feed pumpkins once you see the small fruit developing.
- Check ladybird numbers around your fruit trees to see if they are controlling the green peach aphids that develop on almond, peach and nectarine trees.
- Keep up control methods for codling moth (see p. 109) to prevent the next season's problems.
- Apply a fresh layer of manure and straw around citrus trees. Foliar-feed with trace elements to the entire tree canopy. It will be absorbed through the leaf tissue.
- Plant out celery. It grows in soil with a pH of about 6.0–7.0 and loves lots of water. You can encase them in a 1 litre milk carton to get the stalks to grow tall. Try the variety South Australian Giant.
- Plant spring onions in with dolomite lime and plenty of compost. Don't use animal manures as they will develop bullneck.

- Put blocks of sweet corn in now to harvest in March. The bed should have had lots of manure, compost and hay dug in to make it rich and free-draining. As the corn develops anchor roots, hill them up with more hay and manure. Apply trace elements when the plants are 30 cm tall.

General garden tasks

- Lift any daffodil and jonquil bulbs that did not flower. Do not cut back any of the leaves. Replant them into improved soil with sheep manure and a wetting agent. Apply a liquid fertiliser before the leaves die down.
- Remove any of the frost barriers you have around trees and shrubs so they get full benefit from the spring sunshine.
- Reapply the mulch you removed from around trees and shrubs during the winter months to protect against frost. The soil temperature will start to warm up and plants will need to retain more moisture.
- When reusing pots to grow new plants, clean them with a small amount of bleach and water. Scrub the inside of the pot to get out any remaining dirt. This will prevent soil-borne diseases from infecting the new plants.
- Mulch around berry plants and tie canes as they emerge.

- Replant indoor plants into larger pots if needed. Apply a slow-release fertiliser and refresh the potting mix. Indoor plants can be liquid-fertilised every 3 weeks until the end of summer.
- Replace any lawn that hasn't recovered from the winter frosts. Rake in new soil, lawn-starter fertiliser and either sow seed or lay roll-on.
- Feed clematis to keep them flowering. Never let them dry out and always keep their roots in shade – you can cover the ground with stones or a thick mulch.
- Take cuttings from indoor plants such as figs, dieffenbachia, dracaena and aralia. Place them into a propagation mix in a warm spot until they develop roots.
- Improve sandy soils with clay, compost, manure and wetting agent. Sandy soil is notoriously nutrient-poor and hydrophobic, making it pretty tough for plant growth. Always use a mulch on sandy soils – the evaporation rate is much higher and the soil heats up around root systems.

November

Summer-proofing your garden

Due to climate creep, we are experiencing longer, hotter summertime temperatures. The heat can be relentless in many parts of Australia and rainfall is totally unpredictable. Even the night-time temperatures are becoming warmer with weather patterns bringing stronger winds and storms.

Once daytime temperatures reach above 34 degrees for consecutive days, plants will go into major stress mode – as we do, too. Here's what you can do to help them:

1. Create more upper-canopy shade in your garden, particularly over the vegie patch. Do not use more than 30 per cent shadecloth or the plants will become weak and leggy. Plants that have been recently planted or crisp up every summer can have a shadecloth tent erected around them. This helps keep out the hot winds and reduces evaporation.
2. Apply a wetting agent again to make sure all water delivered is actually getting to the root zone.
3. Mulch – I know, you have heard it a million times, but here I go again. Only use very coarse mulch that water particles can pass through and make it only 5–6 cm thick. All the latest research has found that at 10 cm thick the water does not get down to the root zone (unless there is a torrential downpour

or the retic is on for three times as long). The purpose of mulch is to prevent evaporation, not stop water penetration. Everything in the garden can be mulched, but keep it clear from the trunk of plants to avoid fungal infection.

4. Spray sun-sensitive plants with DroughtShield; it's an acrylic polymer that protects plants from drought, heat, wind, frost and transplant shock. If you are putting new seedlings in at this time of the year, I highly recommend you spray them with DroughtShield first. I spray my fruit trees and more tender plants every year in November and again in February – it lasts for around 90 days. It works a treat for roses that otherwise get that sizzled look.
5. Do not prune fruit trees or heat-sensitive plants during the summer months. This encourages new growth that will be soft and sissy when it comes to temperatures above 34 degrees. The more leaf-cover the better as this provides shade for the plant. The trunk, stems and leaves experience sunburn – you can either put shade cloth around the trunk or paint with a layer of white acrylic paint.
6. Don't panic when your plants wilt. They do this to reduce the amount of sunlight hitting the leaf surface, which reduces transpiration. Wilting is not a bad thing – it's a survival thing. Remember, plants are very clever and have adapted survival mechanisms that we can only dream about. Although I also wilt in the heat.

7. Do not fertilise any stressed plants and certainly do not spray any pest oil or horticultural oil during summer. This will be the equivalent of putting your plants on the BBQ and whipping up a green grill. Fertilising encourages new growth that will succumb to the heat.

It's all mostly common sense – think how we as humans protect ourselves from the heat. I am so thankful I have a garden that has created a cool microclimate around my house.

Peanuts

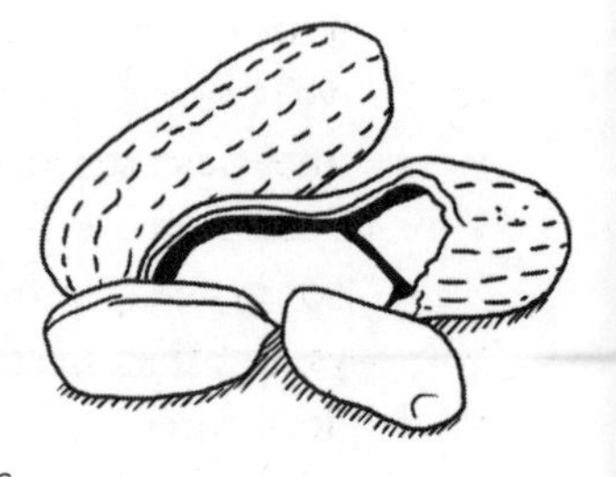

I remember growing peanuts as a kid – it was always so rewarding and exciting to see the size of the crop that a few peanuts could produce. I guess that's why peanuts are one of the world's leading food crops. They are certainly high in protein – the highest per hectare of any food.

The weather in Perth lately has made me think about peanuts because they love the heat and humidity. Peanuts are a long-term crop for the summer as they need four months of heat to grow. It's a great plant to use for crop rotation (see pp. 54–7), putting nitrogen and potassium back into the beds. In northern parts of Australia they plant out at the start of the wet season or November, and harvest at the end of February or March.

Over the past decade there has been a lot of genuine concern about peanut allergies. But if no one in your household is allergic, they are great fun. Kids are absolutely fascinated by the way in which a peanut bush grows.

Go to a health food shop and purchase some raw peanuts, shelled but with the skin on. They are hungry feeders so make sure the beds have compost, manure, trace elements and fertiliser. The soil needs to be friable and free-draining. Plant out the individual nuts 2 cm deep and cover with mulch.

After only one day the nut will have produced a root. It will quickly form a pretty small bush. After four weeks the bush produces gorgeous yellow flowers that are self-pollinating. At flowering time, apply a small handful of gypsum to each bush. The flower only lasts two days and then dies, but what emerges next is the bit kids love.

The dead flower produces a peg that grows down into the soil, and this is where the magic happens – the peanuts are born underground from the peg that dives into the soil. The other exciting thing is that you don't know what's attached until you dig the whole bush up about four months later.

Peanuts MUST be dried out fully before eating. You can do this either by turning the plants upside down and leaving them in the sun for a week, or roasting the nuts in the oven.

Any mouldy peanuts should be discarded immediately – they are toxic.

Pest watch

Do not use pest oil when temperatures are above 34 degrees.

Tomato russet mite will be feeding underneath leaves, stems and fruit on tomato, potato and eggplant bushes. Leaves will become dry, brown and papery. The stems become corky and crack and flowers drop before fruit formation. Powdered sulphur can be used in temperatures below 30 degrees, or rely on predatory mites to wage war against them.

Whitefly is the bane of every garden that grows kale, broccoli and cabbage. They arrive in their thousands because one female will lay up to 200 eggs. The parasitic wasp *Encarsia formosa*, ladybirds, hoverflies and lacewings hook into them and manage to keep the numbers at a manageable level. Yellow sticky strips placed near the plants also work, but may also catch the beneficials. If they are really driving you insane you can resort to spraying with Natrasoap or Eco-Oil if temperatures are below 34 degrees.

All regions

General care

- It's time to move those potted heat-sensitive plants into dappled light or shade. Pots dry out quickly in summer and you will need to water more regularly and apply a wetting agent and mulch to all pots to increase water-holding capacity.

- Check your watering times to ensure plants are receiving enough water and have not grown in front of sprayers, blocking the penetration of water to other plants.
- Remove suckers that are shooting below the graft level of trees. You can rub them off with your fingers or cut them off with a grafting knife.
- Deadhead roses to encourage new blooms and spend time squishing aphids while pruning.
- Spray new growth on roses with a homemade remedy against black spot and powdery mildew. In 1 litre of water, mix 1 teaspoon of bicarb of soda, 3 drops of dishwashing liquid and half a teaspoon of vegetable oil. This can be safely sprayed every few weeks to prevent disease and insects attacking new buds and leaves.
- Feed November lilies before they start dying down. This will ensure enough energy to produce next season's flowers. Once they have completely dried off, remove the dead stems.
- Start thinking about how you will spruce up the garden for the Christmas feasting. Fill up pots with flowering annuals, vegies, herbs and a mixed planting of perennials and annuals.

The edible garden

- Liquid-fertilise all vegies to get them growing fast before the real heat sets in.
- Reinvigorate vegie beds with compost and manure. Dig it into the top 5 cm of soil.

- Apply 1 handful of dolomite lime per square metre to all the vegie beds before planting out new crops.
- Keep building up straw around strawberry plants to keep the fruit off the soil. Feed fortnightly with high-quality liquid fertiliser.
- Spray young cucumber, melon, pumpkin, watermelon and zucchini seedlings with 1 part milk in 5 parts water every week to ward off powdery mildew. Use a small paintbrush to ensure good pollination between flowers (see cucurbit pollination, p. 209).
- Apply your fruit fly control methods (see pp. 172–7) to all your fruit trees and remember to top up traps with a fresh solution every week. Check to see exactly what you are catching in your traps, it will give you an idea of what lives in the garden.
- Clean out crossing and overcrowded branches on citrus trees to improve airflow and sunlight into the centre of the tree.

Natives

- Native groundcovers such as scaevola, brachyscome, kennedia and goodenia can be lightly pruned to encourage continued flowering throughout summer.

- Pot up an Australian native tree for Christmas. Choose a plant that's suitable for your climate and put it in a large pot that can be moved indoors over the Christmas season.

Lawn

- Lift the blades of the mower to a higher level to conserve water and prevent sun scorch. Lawns will need more regular mowing from this month on.
- If your lawn is being infested with weeds it could be a problem with the pH of the soil causing nutrient deficiencies. Spike the lawn with a fork to improve water penetration and drainage.

Pruning

- Finish pruning spring-flowering climbing roses. You can go pretty hard to encourage new flowering canes for next spring.
- Prune protea, leucospermum and banksia by a third. Apply a native slow-release fertiliser.

Planting and cuttings

- Investigate shade trees to plant around your house to cool things down for summer. Visit a tree nursery and select the tree that best suits the area.

- Lift spring-flowering bulbs like hyacinth, tulip and daffodil when the foliage has completely died down (unless you live in high-frost areas). Roll them in sulphur dust and store until autumn next year. (See more on pp. 58–63.)
- Take tip cuttings of anything in your garden that you love and want more of. Try everything – you will have some losses and some wins.

Tropical/Subtropical

Edible garden tasks

- Sow Asian greens, basil, capsicum, chilli, choko, cucumber, eggplant, ginger, lettuce, melon, okra, parsley, pumpkin, rosella, snake beans, spring onion, sweet corn, sweet potato, tomato.
- Banana bunches will start to bulk up and ripening will begin. Feed and flood them every 3 days. (See more on pp. 27–9.)
- Plant a choko vine around the chook pen or over a fence. They grow rapidly and hide untidy areas while shading and feeding the chooks at the same time.
- Spray pawpaw trees with a copper-based spray to control black spot.
- Prune back mango, guava and rambutan trees once they have finished fruiting.
- Keep an eye on pineapples that are ripening. Don't leave them too long on the plant and check for pests.

General garden tasks

- Spray cycads for caterpillar attack with Dipel or Success. Remember to get underneath the fronds.
- Get all the brightly coloured foliaged plants into the ground now it's warming up and the wet season will soon arrive. Croton, ornamental ginger and heliconia can be grown from cuttings or pieces of root.
- Get the compost heap fully activated by adding comfrey and manures to speed up the process. (See more on pp. 25–7.)
- Weeds will start appearing with great enthusiasm. Better to control them now before they seed, even if you just whipper-snip off the heads before they set seed.
- Check to see potted plants are receiving enough moisture. Even though the days are getting more humid, it is still hot and dry.
- Plant out leafy greens in dappled shade from this point on throughout summer or they will bolt to seed. Water in well with a liquid seaweed solution and liquid fertiliser.
- Feed all garden beds with a high potassium fertiliser and seaweed tonic for healthy, disease-free growth.
- Prune wisteria to the fat flowering buds. Wispy long tendrils can be cut right back to the base of the plant.

Temperate/Mediterranean

Edible garden tasks

- Sow Asian greens, basil, beetroot, broccoli, capsicum, carrot, chilli, chives, coriander, cucumber, eggplant, Florence fennel, French beans, leek, lettuce, melon, okra, onion, parsley, potato, pumpkin, radicchio, rocket, spring onion, squash, strawberry, swede, sweet corn, sweet potato, tomato, zucchini.
- Put shadecloth up over vegie gardens now to protect them from the scorching heat. Only use a 30 per cent shadecloth – any more than that and your vegies won't get enough sun.
- Top up mulch on all vegie beds and around fruit trees to prevent evaporation.
- Liquid-fertilise all your vegies to get them growing without stress. You can add seaweed solution at the same time.
- Apply dolomite lime to all fruit trees to alleviate problems with calcium deficiency.
- Place shadecloth screens around the trunks of young fruit trees to protect them from sunburn.
- Apply a wetting agent to hard, dry soils and top with mulch.
- Sow climbing and bush beans directly into ground that has been previously limed and given a good dressing of blood and bone. Allow room for the stakes and don't overcrowd them. Four stakes

tied together gives ample room for them to grow. Keep picking pods as they grow – the more you pick, the more you get.

- Keep layering soil and hay up potato stalks. Drench with a liquid fertiliser mixed with seaweed solution.
- Check that passionfruit vines are getting water to the whole root system. Fertilise and trim back growth that is strangling other plants.
- Put a shadecloth or umbrella over rhubarb plants to keep the leaves from collapsing. Mound up with aged sheep manure and hay.
- Harvest eggplant, cucumber and zucchini when they are young. They will be sweeter and have much more flavour.
- Keep as much foliage on capsicums as possible to protect the fruit from sunburn.

General garden tasks

- Use early mornings or evenings to plant out new shrubs or trees. Make sure the planting hole is wet and remember to mulch. Give new plantings a deep watering every two days for the first week.
- Top up mulch around pots to ensure moisture is retained throughout the entire pot and there is minimal evaporation.
- Soak seedlings in a bucket of seaweed solution before planting into the garden. This will help with transplant shock and keep them moist.

- Roses will need fertilising little and often from now on. Make sure water is getting to the whole root zone and the mulch is sufficient to minimise evaporation.
- Plant your crinum, nerine, lycoris and pineapple lily bulbs.
- Pot up flowering natives that you adore but which won't grow in your soil type. Only use native potting mix and native slow-release fertiliser.
- The NSW Christmas bush (*Ceratopetalum gummiferum*) will be in bud and you will need to ensure it gets enough water for abundant flowering. Do not fertilise the bush until flowering has finished. Give it a light prune and then feed with a native fertiliser.
- The WA Christmas Tree (*Nuytsia floribunda*) will be looking magnificent. For those lucky enough to be able to purchase one from a nursery, they are hemiparasitic and need to be planted with an acacia.
- Lightly prune bougainvillea vines (wearing armour-plated gloves) to encourage summer flowering.
- Give lavender plants a light prune every four weeks. Liquid-fertilise to keep consistent flowering.
- Non-repeat spring-flowering roses can still be pruned before the heat sets in. Remove some of the stems entirely to produce new watershoots for the next season's flowers.

- Go hard at pruning grasses to keep the fresh new growth coming. This can be done with shears or a whipper-snipper. Don't waste the prunings – use them as a mulch.

Cool/Cold

Edible garden tasks

- Sow Asian greens, basil, beetroot, broccoli, carrot, capsicum, chilli, chives, coriander, cucumber, eggplant, endive, Florence fennel, French beans, ginger, leek, lettuce, melon, parsley, parsnip, peas, potato, pumpkin, radicchio, radish, rocket, rosella, silverbeet, spring onion, squash, strawberry, sweet corn, tomato, zucchini.
- Cabbage white butterfly caterpillars can be controlled by spraying Dipel or Success. (See also p. 95.)
- Make sure berry bushes are receiving enough water to develop fruit.
- Grapevines will be putting on masses of growth. Feed them with a granular fertiliser and keep plenty of airflow between canes to prevent downy and powdery mildew from developing on the fruit.
- Apply a mulch around all fruit trees and ensure the water penetrates through the mulch into the ground. Keep mulch away from the trunk of trees.
- Protect all stone fruit from fruit fly with traps, splash baits and netting (see pp. 172–7).

- Prune flowering peaches and cherries to encourage flowering wood for next season. Remove any branches that didn't flower this year. Apply a granular fertiliser after pruning and mulch.
- Thin out stone fruit if it is overcrowded. You will get larger and healthier peaches and nectarines.
- Control summer weeds around fruit trees – they will take nutrients. Slash them down and leave on the ground to put back what they took out.
- Mulberry trees will be flowering or fruiting, depending on the variety. Pick the fruit every day – you won't be able to eat them all but they freeze well and make divine jam. Leave fertilising and pruning until after fruiting.

General garden tasks

- The mountain laurel (*Kalmia latifolia*) is bursting into flower and would have to be one of the most spectacular flowering shrubs for cooler climates.
- Transplant irises after they have finished flowering. Tag them before they die down to identify their colours.
- Plant out summer- and autumn-flowering bulbs like hippeastrums, belladonnas and tuberoses.
- Plant out ornamental onions and cleome for colourful summer flowers.
- Prune back all the spring-flowering shrubs such as lilac, westringia, philadelphus, acacia, deciduous viburnum, forsythia and clematis. Most can be

pruned by a third, otherwise just remove the oldest stems to ground level to keep new stems emerging.

- Cut back protea and leucospermum to keep them compact and improve flowering. After pruning give them a handful of native slow-release fertiliser to encourage side growth.
- Fill in gaps of bare lawn with runners to get them established in the warm weather. Add some compost to the soil before planting and water daily until it is established. Use a lawn-starter fertiliser a week after laying to encourage root growth.
- Lift and divide nerine bulbs once the clumps get so large they are popping out of their pot or from the ground. They will probably sulk for the first year after division, but will reward you with fabulous flowering from the second year.
- Plant the hardwood cuttings you took from your roses, jasmine and honeysuckle plants back in May (see p. 93).
- Lightly prune lavender bushes to get a ripper flowering season.
- Keep planting natives while the soil is warm. Make sure the holes are prepared with compost and a native slow-release fertiliser. Water once or twice a week for their first summer.
- Allow potted cyclamens to dry out and leave in a dry place so they become totally dormant.

December

An aesthetically pleasing vegie patch

Is it possible to have a vegie patch that is the wow-factor of the garden? It most certainly is if you design it creatively and think of vegetables as ornamental as well as functional.

The best approach is to create the design to suit the purpose and then tweak it a bit to maximise aesthetics.

Before embarking on this project I have to make it very clear that if you decide the edible garden is to be the focal point, it requires daily attention. This doesn't always mean work, but certainly observation. There is no such thing as a low-maintenance vegie patch, and people who tell you they only go into their vegie garden once a week for half an hour probably have a garden that looks like it.

Many vegetables are annuals, meaning from germination to harvest takes one season. Leafy greens like lettuce and Asian greens can be harvested within 6 weeks from germination. If you want to get the best from annuals you have to water and feed them regularly.

The other job that needs to be done to keep the edible garden looking fabulous is weed control. Weeds seem to grow at twice the rate of any other plant. This is because they have an advantageous root system and are super efficient at gobbling up water and nutrients at the expense of your prize onion patch. So, to overcome the weed problem you have to make sure there is not enough room for them to grow. Pack your patch.

To get a good harvest you will need to supplement some nutrition in the form of liquid fertilising as well as granular feeding at the beginning of each season. Liquid fertiliser is absorbed by leaf tissue and helps maintain a strong cellular structure. Use a good quality fertiliser that has humic and fulvic acids, to boost not just the plant but also the soil microbes that promote strong root development.

Pay attention to the leaf shape, height and colour of the vegies you choose to grow. Many vegies come in different colours and look great when planted out according to a colour scheme. Lettuce comes in lime green, burgundy, deep green and a combination of all three. Chilli plants have red, black, purple, green, yellow and orange fruit. Cabbages come in purple, green and burgundy. Don't just grow beetroot for its beet, grow it for the foliage – it's great in salads and stir-fry and adds a splash of colour to the garden.

Bear in mind that even an ornamental vegetable garden needs to be planted out according to the plants' nutrient and water needs (see pp. 54–7).

Always incorporate flowers into the edible garden. They serve more than one purpose. Flowers like calendula, marigold and nasturtium are edible too, but they are also good companion plants that ward off pests and attract beneficial insects. Lobelia, alyssum, salvia, verbena and poppy will bring in predatory insects, and small insectivore birds will relish knocking off the sap-suckers in the garden.

Rainbow chard has sensational colours on the stems – yellow, pink, red, green, purple and white. I actually use them throughout the garden as they are architectural as well as edible.

Bounce flower colour off leaf colour, mix blue lobelia with purple cabbages, yellow marigold with orange capsicums, red dahlias with tomatoes. It fills the garden space with a kaleidoscope of colour.

The site of the vegie patch is very important, as you want it to look good all year round. Nearly all vegies need 6 hours of sun a day. If they grow in too much shade they will be weak and have spindly growth. A half-dead tomato or English spinach patch gives the wrong sort of wow-factor. Use climbing frames for beans and zucchini to add height to the garden.

Edible gardens should also have sculptural elements. You can use recycled materials and make it a family heirloom. It could become an annual project. Always include some type of creative project that gives your garden a personal touch. Then it becomes more than just a vegie patch – it's a statement about self-sufficiency, creativity and the joy of playing with nature.

Growing cucurbits

The warmer months are definitely the time to get your cucurbits into the ground. No, it's not your old smelly sock pile, but the melon family.

Temperatures above 15 degrees will be needed for germination to be successful.

Notable members of the cucurbit family include watermelon, pumpkin, cucumber, zucchini, squash, marrow and rock melon.

Most cucurbits are annuals and are much better planted directly into the soil from seed, as they hate root disturbance. The great thing about annual vegetables is that they mature quickly. The seed is large and flat so it's a great starter plant for kids and novice adult gardeners.

Soil preparation, planting and watering

Any fruit-producing annual will need lots of good nutrients and ample moisture in the ground. Good drainage is essential for this whole family, as is good quality compost, manure and mulch. Although most of us have had experience with a rabid pumpkin taking over the back yard and growing on neglect, a good source of nitrogen is essential for good cropping.

It is best to prepare the area for growing a few weeks before planting out the seed. Mix in equal parts of chicken manure with compost and 2 handfuls of blood and bone with trace elements.

In free-draining sandy soils, make a well around each seed so that water collects around the root base. If you live in an area with heavier clay soils, you will need to do the opposite and mound the plants up to assist drainage. Always sow two or three seeds in the one hole and then remove the weakest.

Most of the cucurbit family has large leaves that transpire lots of water and often wilt during the hottest part of the day. If you are planting out the softer fruits such as cucumber in midsummer, you may need to give them afternoon shade.

Mulching is vital to the health of the plant and prevents evaporation around the root system. You will need it at least 15 cm thick. I like to use lupin mulch, but pea straw or lucerne hay is just as good.

Avoid overhead watering as this may encourage powdery mildew, which can be a bit of a problem with some of the cucurbit family. If you have to water with overhead sprinklers, do it early in the morning so the water evaporates before the heat of the day hits the leaves. When temperatures reach over 34 degrees you may need to water cucurbits twice a day depending on the site and soil type.

Flowering and pollinating

It appears that the male flowers want to jump the gate long before the females come off the dance floor. In the melon family, it's usually the male flowers that appear first. They will be attached to long stems that grow into the leaf canopy with a rod-like stamen in the middle of the flower. The female will have a round lump below the petals and grow close to the main stem.

Unless you have many bees around, you will need to hand-pollinate the flowers yourself. However, you must pollinate the female flowers while they are closed or semi-closed for success. This needs to be done early in the morning. You'll need one male flower for every four females. Pull the petals off the male flower and tickle the stamen inside the female flower.

Pumpkin, marrow and squash

These are warm-season, frost-tender vine crops with fruit of various sizes, shapes, colours and intensity of flavours.

Pumpkin, marrow and squash need plenty of organic material added to the soil to aid fertilisation and fruit set.

Once fruits reach golf-ball size, apply additional all-purpose fertiliser around the root zone.

Pumpkins are best planted in full sun in pairs, 40–50 cm apart. They will reach maturity around 3–4 months later. Start harvesting when the vine begins to die back. When you cut your pumpkin off the vine, always leave a 10 cm stalk and store in a dry area with good air circulation. This will prevent disease entering the pumpkin.

Marrow and squash mature sooner. They are more compact and can be grown up a trellis.

Prescott Fond Blanc (heirloom)

Dates back to 1850s. Sweet orange juicy flesh.

Turk's Turban

Has a little knob on top with orange, white and green strips.

Butternut

Long and delicious. Fruits better in warm climates.

Atlantic Giant

The giant pumpkin that can reach up to 220 kg.

Delicata Bush Mini

The dwarf little pumpkin that tastes similar to sweet potato.

Jap

Soft skin and compact fruit. No one's really sure if the name comes from 'Japanese' or 'Just Another Pumpkin'.

Rockmelon

Rockmelon seeds are best planted at 120 cm apart and mounded up. They will need regular watering to start them off and during flowering, but be careful not to overwater once the melons start to reach half their size as this may cause rotting.

Plant the seeds direct 3–5 cm deep in free-draining soil. Seeds will germinate in 5–10 days and rockmelons will be ready for harvest in around 12 weeks.

French Charentais (heirloom)

Orange flesh. Good for cooler climates.

Mini Melon Minnesota

Dwarf melon 10 cm in size, but makes up for it with the flavour. Grows on a 1 metre vine and is wilt-resistant.

Nutmeg

Sweet greenish flesh. Suitable for cooler climates.

Ha'Ogen

Sweet, fragrant and compact in growth.

Cucumber

Cucumber is a warm-season vine that can be trained up a trellis or left as a groundcover. They will need temperatures above 24 degrees to set fruit.

Cucumbers prefer soil that is very free-draining. They

develop a deep root system and will need ample water and liquid fertilising until the cucumbers are well formed.

Plant seeds about 2 cm deep and space them 2.5 metres apart. Always cut back the main leaders to encourage the development of female flowers. You will be harvesting within 7 weeks.

Spacemaster

Stocky little cucumber with 20 cm sized fruits.

Armenian Burpless

Ribbed skin and yellow flesh with huge yields.

Lebanese

Mediterranean variety with long, thin fruit and large yields.

Revel

Mildew- and virus-resistant with long dark-green fruit.

Watermelon

What kid wouldn't want to grow watermelons? There is something wonderful about a vine-ripened melon that has all the natural sugars peaking.

Thankfully there is quite a variety of watermelons available now, including the fabulous compact Sugar Baby. These smaller melons hardly take up any room in the vegie bed and are quick to mature.

Plant the seeds 4 cm deep. Space 3 metres apart for full-sized melons, or 1.5 metres apart for the compact variety. From seed to harvest is around 11 weeks.

Moon and Stars (heirloom)

Delicious sweet red flesh with speckled skin.

Golden Midget (heirloom)

Little compact grower and suitable for cooler climates. Takes only 80 days to harvest and the skin turns a golden honey colour with sweet red flesh.

Sugar Baby

Small green fruit on a compact shrub.

Zucchini

Zucchini has the reputation of being the idiot-proof vegetable. Apparently they will grow in spite of the worst black-thumbed gardener. They're great for gardeners who want instant gratification as from seed to the first harvest is only 5 weeks. You can almost see zucchinis grow. Don't leave them on the vine too long, though, as they get so tough you could use them as surfboard filler.

Black Beauty

Bushy plant with heavy fruit set.

Gold Finger

Smooth golden fruit and a heavy harvest.

Gold Rush

Early grower that is suitable for cooler climates.

Pest watch

Do not use pest oil when temperatures are above 34 degrees.

Use this month to discover more about all the insects that visit your garden. Take a magnifying glass out each morning to see what's happening behind the leaves.

Watch to see what birds come to visit and what they eat. Nearly all birds eat insects and some use cobwebs to help build their nests.

Think of your garden as a habitat for all species. If you live in the city, it may be the only place where they can find a small patch of nature.

All regions

General care

- Get dirty in the garden in the early morning or late afternoon – you will enjoy it much more than wilting in the midday sun.
- Spray susceptible plants with a polymer coating like DroughtShield to prevent sunburn and excess transpiration.
- Compost will dry out quickly over the next few months, so make sure you give it a light watering twice a week. It should have the moisture of a squeezed sponge. Keep a cover over it to deter flies and keep the heat inside.

- Make sure potted plants are receiving enough moisture. If the water runs straight through, you will need to apply a wetting agent and water in really well. Every third year, remove a third of the potting mix and refresh with new potting mix and compost.
- All timber outdoor furniture should be re-oiled to prevent it from drying out and bleaching. Hose all outdoor furniture down and check for spiders that may have made their home in crevices.
- Have an arborist check the integrity of any large trees that surround your house. Summer storms can cause limb drop.
- Prepare the garden if you are going away over the Christmas break. Go through everything that needs watering and check to make sure the reticulation system is working on all sprinklers and drippers. Give the garden a really good soak before leaving. Group potted plants together in the shade to make the job easier for the person looking after the garden in your absence.

The edible garden

- Erect shadecloth over vegie beds to prevent sun scorch and heat stress that will cause plants to bolt to seed. Some vegies such as tomato and eggplant will actually get sunscald and dry out entirely.

- Spray all the cucurbit family with 1 part milk to 5 parts water to prevent powdery mildew developing on leaves.
- Keep building up straw around strawberry plants to keep the fruit off the soil. Feed fortnightly with high quality liquid fertiliser.
- Plant out tropical trees so they get well established before the winter arrives. Enrich the planting hole and apply a 6 cm thick mulch.
- Lightly fertilise citrus trees that have small fruit developing. Keep the mulch at a depth of 5 cm and make sure it isn't in contact with the trunk.
- Passionfruit vines and grapevines can be lightly pruned now to prevent them from taking over the whole garden.

Lawn

- Apply a light dressing of compost and a complete lawn fertiliser to have your lawn looking great for Christmas. Water it in well and mow regularly.

Pruning

- Deadhead rose bushes and make sure they are getting adequate water. Apply a wetting agent if necessary and water in thoroughly.
- Prune back melaleuca and callistemon that have finished flowering. You can safely take a third off all branches.

- Prune off kangaroo paw flowers 10 cm from the base of the plant. They make fantastic vase flowers and last for weeks. The yellow and red ones give the house a Christmassy look.

Planting and cuttings

- Soak all seedlings in a tub with seaweed solution. The whole punnet can be dipped in to cover the entire plant. This will help alleviate transplant shock.
- Make up pots of flowering annuals to have at the entrance of paths and patios to brighten the place up for Christmas. Overplant them to get the most impact.
- Choose a sunny spot to plant out lots of sunflowers. They cheer up gardeners and garden visitors.
- Take cuttings of daphne plants. Use only propagation mix and keep them in a shady cool spot.

Tropical/Subtropical

Edible garden tasks

- Sow Asian greens, basil, capsicum, chilli, choko, cucumber, eggplant, ginger, lettuce, melon, okra, parsley, rosella, snake beans, spring onion, sweet corn, sweet potato, sword beans, tomato.

- Direct sow summer vegies into beds. They will develop faster and have a deeper root system. Keep them clear of mulch until the seedlings emerge.
- Keep successive plantings of corn, beans and tomatoes happening in the garden to have a constant supply of fresh vegies over the wet season.
- Keep baiting for fruit fly (see pp. 172–7) by placing traps on trees and spraying with spinosad.
- Protect banana, lychee, pawpaw and rambutan fruit from fruit bats by placing exclusion bags over fruit. If you use netting over the entire tree, choose wildlife-friendly netting that is white and densely woven, to prevent the bats from becoming entangled.
- Feed up banana plants with aged chicken manure and compost and water regularly. (See more on pp. 27–9.)
- Pawpaw fruit that has black spot on the skin will need to be soaked in hot water to kill off the fungus.
- Tip-prune guava trees to keep them fruiting throughout the wet season. Harvest the fruit before it ripens to avoid fungal spot.
- Dragon fruit will be flowering now – the perfume from the flowers at night is divine. They need lots of compost and moist conditions. The plants need to be supported by a trellis. Keep tying the stems to the trellis at a height that you can reach the fruit.

General garden tasks

- Push some waterlily fertiliser tablets into pots to encourage summer flowering (see p. 15). Waterlilies can also be lifted and divided up.
- If you've got waterlilies, why not try growing lotus as well? This time of year, lotus plants are beginning to sprout and you can propagate them by cutting the root into 20–30 cm sections and potting up into an aquatic potting mix with 3 cm of gravel on top and placing back into the pond. The new shoots are also delicious to eat in a stir-fry or salad.
- Move delicate plants into a more protected area in preparation for storms or heavy rainfall.
- Take cuttings from cordyline, ixora, plectranthus, frangipani, coleus and croton. They will develop roots quickly in the hot weather.
- Granular fertilise lawn but don't mow too short. This will be the last time you fertilise until the beginning of the dry season.
- Containers that fill up with water over the wet season become a breeding ground for mosquitoes. Avoid this by moving all containers.
- Prune tamarillo bushes if they have become straggly by taking a third off branches.

Temperate/Mediterranean

Edible garden tasks

- Sow Asian greens, basil, capsicum, chilli, coriander, cucumber, eggplant, French beans, ginger, lettuce, melon, okra, onion, parsley, pumpkin, snake beans, squash, sweet corn, sweet potato, tomato, zucchini.
- You will need to apply dolomite lime to tomato, capsicum, eggplant and zucchini seedlings to ensure they have enough calcium and magnesium for robust growth.
- Ensure vegies and citrus trees are getting regular watering. This will help to prevent fruit splitting. Make sure all vegie beds are well mulched.
- Keep harvesting strawberries daily and give a fortnightly feed of a liquid fertiliser. Control slaters with diatomaceous earth sprinkled at the base of plants (see p. 160).
- Hill up sweet corn plants as they grow. The aerial roots will anchor them in the soil and access more nutrients and water.
- Many of the leafy greens will bolt to seed at this time of the year in heat spikes or if they are water stressed.
- Save the seed from this season's vegie crop. Store them in a glass jar, label and keep in a cool place for planting out later in the year. Saved seed will acclimatise better each year.

General garden tasks

- Check trees for signs of borer – you will see branches dying back or leaves going yellow. Look for small amounts of sawdust that will lead you to the hole. Prune off the branches and dispose.
- Evergreen magnolias and michelias will need a boost to cope with the hot months. Dig in some compost and cow manure around the drip line. Apply a pine bark or sheoak mulch, a wetting agent and iron chelates to maintain their health. Deep watering every 3–4 days is better than daily light watering.
- Foliar-feed all plants early in the morning with a spray pack. There are many liquid solutions that can target plant nutrient deficiencies or an all-rounder trace element solution. This works particularly well for citrus plants that are suffering from an iron and magnesium deficiency.
- Move hanging baskets away from hot, drying winds into a more protected area.
- Spray trees with a polymer coating like DroughtShield to protect them from sunburn.
- Give lawns a light covering of compost. Apply a wetting agent and don't mow too short – a bit of length will protect the roots from the heat.
- Pot up plants to give as gifts at Christmas time.

Cool/Cold

Edible garden tasks

- Sow Asian greens, basil, beetroot, broccoli, capsicum, carrot, chilli, chives, cucumber, eggplant, endive, ginger, Florence fennel, French beans, leek, lettuce, melon, parsley, parsnip, peas, potato, pumpkin, rosella, spring onion, silverbeet, squash, sweet corn, tomato, zucchini.
- Dig broad bean plants into the ground to add nitrogen to the soil.
- Prune blackcurrant bushes when they finish flowering. Apply trace elements to other berry plants that are still fruiting.
- Keep up with good hygiene in the orchard. Pick up fallen fruit, get the chooks in there to clean up fruit fly larvae and keep replacing the baits in traps (see pp. 172–7).
- Fill gaps underneath fruit trees with low-growing herbs like oregano and thyme. These herbs love the summer heat and will keep a cool root run.
- Use as much greywater on fruit trees as possible to conserve water. Always use greywater-friendly products and move the water to different areas each week.

General garden tasks

- Compost horse and sheep manure with hay before putting into garden beds. The heat will kill off weed seeds.
- Prune back delphiniums when flowering has finished to have a second flush of flowers in the autumn months.
- Fertilise autumn-flowering natives after a light prune.
- Garden beds that have been taken over by weeds can have a total revamp. Apply a thick layer of manure and cover with clear plastic to cook the weeds and their seeds. By the end of summer you can remove the covering, add dolomite lime and mulch, ready to plant out the next crop.
- Areas of lawn that don't thrive because of lack of sunshine can be replaced with paving for a small table and chair, turning a dead space into a usable space.
- Make use of the hot days to propagate plants by aerial layering, cuttings or collecting dried seed.
- Hydrangeas and gardenias will need extra watering during December. Apply a liquid fertiliser every fortnight and deadhead them as the flowers die down.
- Lightly prune jasmine after flowering has finished to keep the vine more compact.
- Put your feet up and plan what you want to do in the garden next year.

Acknowledgements

I am a believer in community. Community can only be created when people have a deep respect for each other and acknowledge the talents and commitment of each individual. I have been blessed with being part of the Fremantle Press community, and I need to thank Naama Amram, my eternally patient editor, who persisted gently to get my bum into gear to finish this book. Also, a big thank you to Tracey Gibbs, who again showed her talents as a designer and illustrator. In an era of dwindling publishing houses I feel very proud to be an author with Fremantle Press – it's exceptional.

About Sabrina

Sabrina Hahn is a horticultural expert, radio presenter, podcaster, tour guide and writer. She has a passion for the creation of sustainable environments and livable cities. She believes everyone's garden, regardless of size, plays a vital role in returning biodiversity into cities and offering people a space for physical and mental wellbeing.

Her extensive knowledge on gardening comes from a scientific background of horticulture, soil science, entomology and botany. Sabrina has been awarded a lifetime membership of Nursery and Garden Industry Western Australia and was nominated for Australian of the Year for her services to the industry.

Sabrina has travelled the world leading gardening tours for Australians Studying Abroad and translating the philosophy of those gardens into the Australian landscape.

Sabrina has worked extensively for the past decade in remote Aboriginal communities in the Kimberley, enabling local people to become more self-sufficient and helping to improve the health of children and adults. She has formed friendships with women elders in communities to enable them to propagate their own bush tucker and bush medicine plants so that their knowledge is passed onto the next generation.

sabrinahahn.com.au

 /hortwithheart

 @sshahn1

 @sabrinahahnhortwithheart

A-Z index

T = Tropical/Subtropical zone
M = Temperate/Mediterranean zone
C = Cool/Cold zone

abelias 33, 46, 105, 125
abutilons 20, 30
aeoniums 12
African violets 36
agapanthus 33, 50, 67, 156, 182
ageratum 163
aglaonemas 156
allamandas 182
alliums 52, 92, 93
almonds 117, 128, 185
alstroemerias 63
alyssum 86, 205
Amazon lily 140
anemones 52, 60, 62, 90
angelicas 108
annuals 32–3, 33, 46, 50, 90, 91, 108, 125, 146, 179, 217
anthracnose 47
anti-transpirants 129
  see also DroughtShield
ants 17, 37, 99, 137
aphids 16, 95, 106, 137, 154, 163, 171, 184, 185
apples 21, 37, 66, 73, 84, 106, 109, 117, 118, 122
apricots 72, 117, 119, 122
aralia 187
arbutus 11
ardisias 127
armyworms 63–4
arrowroot 35
artichokes 92
  T 18, 123
  M 70, 88, 105, 126, 143, 160
  C 91, 108, 128, 145, 162, 184
artificial turf 150
Asian greens 83, 204
  T 34, 47, 67, 86, 103, 123, 141, 157, 180, 196, 217
  M 21, 88, 143, 160, 182, 198, 220
  C 23, 38, 72, 184, 201, 222
  see also Ceylon spinach; Chinese cabbage
asparagus 42–4
  T 103, 123, 124, 141, 157
  M 70, 88, 105, 126, 143, 160
  C 72, 91, 108, 128, 145, 162
asparagus ferns 89
assassin bugs 63
asters 110, 123
avocados 19, 45, 47, 87, 98, 117, 158
azalea lace bugs 171
azaleas 18, 20, 33, 37, 39, 50, 147, 171, 178, 184

babacos 141
babianas 90
bamboos 62–3, 181
bananas 18–19, 27–9, 35, 47, 117, 158, 180, 196, 218
banksias 65, 71, 81, 84, 99, 102, 125, 127, 156, 195
Barbados cherries 158
basil 92,
  sowing 157
  T 18, 22, 34, 47, 67, 86, 103, 123, 141, 157, 180, 181, 196, 217
  M 88, 143, 160, 182, 198, 220
  C 38, 201, 222
beans 45, 55, 57
  bush 198–9
  climbing 67, 198–9
  T 18, 218
  M 21, 36, 49, 143, 160
  C 23, 128
  see also broad beans; French beans; snake beans; sword beans
beer traps 29, 81, 178
bees, and diatomaceous earth 160
beetroot 55, 205
  companion planting 128
  T 47, 86, 103, 123, 141
  M 18, 21, 36, 49, 70, 143, 160, 198
  C 23, 38, 51, 72, 162, 201, 222
begonias
  bedding 90
  powdery mildew in 20
  tuberous 24, 36, 62, 140
belladonnas 60, 202
berry plants 21, 70, 186, 201
  see also specific berries, e.g. raspberries
billardieras 183
bindii 101
birdbaths 18, 125, 158
birds
  attracting 51, 84, 125, 144
  eating fruit 19, 35, 104, 126

birds *continued*
as pollinators 100
as predators 63, 64, 206, 214
black spot 69, 193
blackcurrants 38, 72, 92, 222
blood and bone 129, 138–9
blossom-end rot 54
bluebells 52, 59, 90
blueberries 131–3
blueberry ash 127
blueing tonic 145, 155, 162
borax 143
Bordeaux mix 106
borers 16, 81, 85, 221
boron 55
boronias 52, 144, 183
botrytis 169
bottlebrush trees *see* callistemons
bouganvilleas 20, 48, 183, 200
box 46
boysenberries 21, 70
brachyscome daisies 88, 194
brambleberries 70
brassica family 51, 54, 71, 86, 94–5, 143
broad beans 55, 83
T 47, 67, 86, 103, 123
M 88, 105
C 51, 72, 91–2, 108–9, 128, 145, 222
broccoli 94–5
pests and diseases 192
T 18, 47, 67, 86, 103, 123
M 21, 49, 70, 88, 105, 126, 182, 198
C 23, 38, 51, 72, 91, 108, 128, 145, 162, 184, 201, 222
broccolini 94
bromeliads 33, 142, 155
bronze orange bugs 106, 120
brown rot 24, 37, 128
brugmansias 33, 123
brunfelsias 135
brussels sprouts 23, 38, 51, 72, 91, 94–5, 108
buddleias 32, 33, 46, 52, 90, 163
budworms 104, 125
bulbs 59, 90, 93, 144, 200
autumn-flowering 23, 30, 36, 39, 202
poisonous to dogs 135
spring-flowering 39, 50, 52, 58–63, 177, 196
summer-flowering 108, 140, 144, 164, 179, 202
see also specific bulbs, e.g. nerines
butterflies 99

cabbage white butterflies 54, 63, 81, 87, 95, 201
cabbages 57, 71, 94–5, 205
pests and diseases 192
T 18, 34, 47, 67, 86
M 21, 36, 49, 70
C 23, 38, 51, 72, 145, 162
caladiums 20, 48, 88, 125, 142
calendulas 33, 91, 205
callistemons 71, 90, 137, 162, 183, 216
camellia mites 121
camellias 18, 37, 39, 50, 105, 121, 123, 144, 184
campanulas 67
candytufts 91, 102, 125
cannas 62–3, 69, 88
Cape gooseberries 18, 34
cape lilac moths 171–2
cape lilacs 11
capsicums 199, 220
T 18, 34, 157, 180, 196, 217
M 182, 198, 220
C 23, 201, 222
carnations 146
carob trees 118
carrots 57, 160
companion planting 128
T 67, 86, 103, 123, 141, 157, 160, 180
M 36, 49, 70, 126, 143, 182, 198
C 23, 38, 51, 72, 108, 145, 162, 184, 201, 222
cassava 47, 67, 86, 87, 181
caterpillars 44, 171–2, 197
see also armyworms; budworms; cabbage white butterflies; webbing caterpillars
catmint 67
cauliflowers 23, 38, 47, 49, 67, 70, 91, 95, 108, 184
ceanothus 163
celeriac 51
celery
T 47, 67, 86, 103, 123
M 36, 49, 70, 88, 143, 160
C 72, 91, 145, 162, 185
Ceylon spinach 34
chamomile 128
cherries 38, 49, 117, 118
chervil 108
chickens *see* chooks
chill factor 104, 119, 131
chillies 205
T 18, 34, 157, 180, 196, 217
M 182, 198, 220
C 72, 201, 222

Chinese cabbage
T 18, 34, 47, 67, 86, 103, 123, 141, 157
M 36, 49, 70, 88, 105, 126, 143, 160
Chinese celery 83
chives
T 18, 34, 47, 67, 86, 103, 123, 141, 157, 180
M 21, 36, 49, 88, 105, 126, 143, 160, 182, 198
C 23, 38, 51, 184, 201, 222
choisyas 33, 46
chokos 123, 141, 143, 157, 180, 196, 217
chooks 36, 64, 173, 196, 222
Christmas 193, 195, 215, 221
Christmas bush (NSW) 200
Christmas tree (WA) 200
chrysanthemums 129, 156
cinerarias 85
cinnamon 48
citrus 11, 19, 68, 71, 106, 122, 183
feeding and fertilising 36, 45, 84, 139, 161, 185, 216, 221
pests and diseases 16, 34, 81, 100, 106, 120, 124, 139
potted 51
pruning 19, 145, 194
watering 34, 220
citrus bud mites 100
citrus gall wasps 16, 106, 139
citrus leaf miners 81
clay soils 91
clematis 164, 202
cleomes 202
climate change 8
climate zones 8–10
climbers 37, 66, 69, 183
clivias 34, 156, 179
cloches 109
cocoyams 35
codling moths 21, 34, 109, 139, 185
coffee 87
coleus 156, 219
comfrey 197
companion planting 49, 128, 205
compost 19, 25–7, 30, 32, 35, 36, 139, 177, 197, 214
conostylis 88
coprosmas 12
cordylines 48, 156, 219
coreopsis 67
coriander 92, 157
T 86, 103, 123, 141, 157, 180
M 70, 88, 126, 143, 160, 182, 198, 220
C 72, 91, 92, 128, 145, 162, 184, 201
corms 60–2
corn see sweet corn
cornflowers 49, 52, 85, 125, 163
correas 52, 71, 84, 144
cosmos 102, 125, 146, 163, 179
cotoneasters 171
couch grass 151
crabapples 51, 161, 171
crepe myrtles 20, 142
cress
T 18, 34, 47, 67, 86, 103
M 21, 36, 49, 70, 88, 105, 126
C 23
crinums 34, 200
crocuses 39, 52, 90, 179
crop rotation 47, 49, 51, 54–7
crotons 156, 197, 219
cucumbers 22, 23, 57, 199, 207, 208, 211–12
pests and diseases 20, 63, 180–1, 194
T 34, 67, 141, 157, 180–1, 196, 217
M 18, 36, 182, 198, 220
C 23, 184, 201, 222
cucurbit plants 22, 57, 180–1, 194, 207–13, 216
curl grubs 63–4
currants 23
curry bushes 46
custard apples 87, 124, 141
cuttings
hardwood 93, 108, 202
indoor plants 187
tip 18, 196
cycads 33, 127–8, 197
cyclamens 37, 53, 62, 164, 202
cymbidiums 24, 30, 65, 90, 183

daffodils 50, 59, 90, 93, 186, 196
dahlias 24, 66, 72, 74, 156, 179, 184
powdery mildew in 20
tree 67, 123, 142
daikons 67, 70, 72, 86, 88, 91
daisies 33, 46, 57, 88, 110, 140, 156, 194
daphnes 33, 46, 108, 109, 155, 217
Davidson's plum 87
day lilies 67, 105
deciduous trees 11, 83, 122–3, 129
delphiniums 93, 108, 223

desert rose 159
dianellas 33, 46, 67
dianthus 46, 67, 123
diatomaceous earth 17, 49, 160, 220
dieffenbachias 187
dill 72, 86, 88, 91, 105, 126, 143, 160, 162, 184
Dipel (caterpillar spray) 44, 95, 125
diseases *see* specific diseases, e.g. powdery mildew
dog-friendly gardens 134–6
dracaenas 48, 187
dragon fruits 35, 48, 87, 141, 218
dragonflies 16
DroughtShield (anti-transpirant) 37, 129, 189, 214, 221
drumstick trees 35, 48, 159
durantas 18

edible garden *see* vegie patches
eggplant 31, 72, 199, 215, 220
  pests and diseases 192
  T 18, 34, 67, 141, 157, 180, 196, 217
  M 21, 36, 160, 182, 198, 220
  C 184, 201, 222
elderberries 117, 125
endive
  T 47, 67
  M 49, 70, 105, 126, 143
  C 38, 72, 91, 108, 128, 145, 162, 184, 201, 222
English spinach 57, 84
  T 47, 67, 86, 103, 123, 141, 157
  M 88, 105, 126, 143
  C 38, 51, 72, 91, 108, 128, 145, 162, 184
epiphytic orchids 155
eremophilas 12
eriostemons 52, 144
eucalypt trees 13, 81, 99, 146, 178
eucharis lilies 20
euonymus 127
euphorbias 12
exclusion bags 94, 173, 177, 218

feijoas 117
ferns 39, 45, 87, 89, 143
fertilisers 154, 155, 164, 190, 197, 205
figs 19, 45, 104, 117, 187
fire-resistant gardens 11–13
flax 67
Florence fennel
  T 47, 103, 180
  M 70, 88, 143, 160, 182, 198
  C 51, 72, 108, 162, 184, 201, 222
flower set 87
flowering cherry 109, 126, 202
flowering peach 126, 202
flowering plum 126
flowering quince 126, 171
flowers 52, 85, 102
  in vegie patch 49, 86, 156, 160, 205
  see also annuals; perennials; pollination; specific flowers, e.g. pansies
foliar feeding 47, 158, 161, 180, 185, 221
forsythias 202
foxgloves 33, 108
frangipanis 12, 36, 48, 125, 158, 219
freesias 52, 59, 62, 90
French beans
  T 86, 103, 123, 141, 157, 180
  M 182, 198, 220
  C 184, 201, 222
frost-burn 146
frosts 72, 73, 93, 109, 129, 146
fruit bats 19, 35, 100, 180, 218
fruit fly 172–7
  baits 29, 49, 176
  control measures 177, 194, 218
  trapping 174–5
fruit trees 45, 49, 104, 105, 106, 108, 198, 201, 202, 222
  chill factor 104
  feeding and fertilising 38, 47, 89, 143, 161
  pests and diseases 49, 70, 72–3, 104, 121, 139, 172–7, 185, 201
  pollination 104, 117–19
  propagating and grafting 65, 139
  pruning 19, 21, 24, 32, 37, 84, 110, 189
  rootstock 82
  thinning crop 66, 182, 202
  T 87, 124, 180
  C 128
  see also specific fruits, e.g. apricots
fuchsias 105
fungal diseases 19
  see also specific diseases, e.g. powdery mildew
fungicides 10

galangal 18, 34, 48
galanthus 59
galls 85

galtonias 164
gardenias 18, 30, 33, 36, 46, 147, 178, 223
garlic 70, 72, 78–81, 86, 88, 91, 103, 105, 108, 123, 126, 128
gauras 67
gazanias 156
Geraldton wax 144, 183
geraniums 18, 33, 90
gerberas 22, 67, 90
geums 91, 163
ginger 20, 48, 62–3, 68, 69, 88, 89, 142
ornamental 197
T 18, 34, 180, 181, 196, 217
M 220
C 201, 222
gladioli 62, 144, 179
gloriosas 179
goodenias 194
gooseberries 23, 163
grapefruit *see* citrus
grapevines 21, 32, 84, 106, 121, 124, 128, 161, 201, 216
grasses 107, 183, 200
green manure crops 55, 83
grevilleas 33, 52, 65, 85, 125, 183
greywater 126–7, 222
groundcovers 194
guavas 117, 196, 218
gum trees *see* eucalypt trees
gutters 36, 64, 177
gymea lilies 90, 178
gypsophilas 146
gypsum 79, 91, 120, 191

haemanthus 60
hakeas 33, 52, 65
hand-pollination 22, 194, 209
hanging baskets 85, 179, 221
hardenbergias 144, 183
harpephyllums 11
hawthorn trees 49, 51, 127
hazelnuts 128
heat-proofing 188–90, 192, 198–9
hebes 33
hedges 32, 36, 46, 65, 156, 183
heliconias 48, 69, 88, 197
hellebores 107, 110, 135
hens *see* chooks
herbs 65, 92, 109, 163, 193, 222
see also specific herbs, e.g. coriander
hibiscus 140, 159, 183
hibiscus beetles 29
hippeastrums 20, 34, 60, 105, 140, 144, 202
holly 135
hollyhocks 52, 102
honeydew secretions 137
honeysuckles 93, 203
hostas 24
house plants *see* indoor plants
hoverflies 184, 192
hyacinths 50, 52, 59, 60, 90, 196
hydrangeas
blueing tonic 145, 155, 162
fertilising 145, 163, 223
poisonous to dogs 135
powdery mildew in 22
pruning 66, 90, 105, 163

impatiens 36
indoor plants 30, 52, 73, 82, 107, 155, 164, 183, 187
insecticides 10, 149, 174, 176
insects 10, 16, 35, 81, 156, 214
attracting beneficial 49, 86, 90, 125, 137, 144, 156, 160, 184, 205
and diatomaceous earth 160
and pollination 97–100
predatory 148–9, 156, 184, 192, 205
see also specific insects, e.g. hoverflies
ipheions 90
irises 52, 62, 164, 202
bearded 23, 24, 89
Dutch 59, 90
Louisiana 23
native (*Patersonia*) 103
iron chelates 36, 85, 178, 221
ixias 52, 90
ixoras 36, 219

Japanese flowering quinces 126
jasmines 93, 203, 223
Jerusalem artichokes 57
M 88, 105, 126, 143, 160
C 91, 108, 128, 145, 162
jonquils 52, 59, 186

kalanchoes 12
kale 51, 56–7, 95
pests and diseases 44, 192
T 47, 86, 103, 141
M 49, 70–1, 88, 105, 126, 143, 160
C 23, 72, 91, 184
kangaroo paws 66, 178, 217

kennedia 194
kiwifruit 89, 128, 144
knees 23
kohlrabi 57, 94, 103, 105, 124
T 18, 86, 103
M 21, 70, 88, 105
C 23, 72, 162, 184
kumquats 89

laburnums 109
lacewings 148, 149, 154, 192
ladybirds 44, 63, 137, 141, 185
lamb's ear 12, 156
larkspurs 102, 146
lavender 18, 22, 33, 46, 49, 200, 203
lawns 12, 22, 31–2, 45, 52, 71, 85, 102, 107, 149–53
fertilising 151, 164, 187, 203, 216, 219, 221
fungal diseases 32, 139
moss in 38, 69, 107
mowing 22, 52, 71, 145, 151, 164, 195, 219, 221
varieties 152–3
weeds in 101, 122, 195
layering, propagation by 147
leaf blister mites 121
leaf-eating ladybirds 63
leafy greens 31, 163, 197, 204, 220
see also specific plants, e.g. lettuce
leaves, as mulch 82, 110, 138
leeks 57, 92
T 18, 47, 67, 86, 103
M 21, 36, 49, 70, 88, 160, 182, 198
C 23, 38, 51, 72, 91, 184, 201, 222
lemongrass 18, 34, 87, 107, 142, 181
lemons *see* citrus
lettuce 31, 57, 204, 205
T 47, 67, 86, 103, 123, 141, 157, 180, 196, 217
M 49, 70, 88, 105, 126, 143, 160, 182, 198, 220
C 23, 38, 51, 145, 162, 184, 201, 222
leucojums 59
leucospermums 195, 203
lilacs 93, 202
lilies 90
liliums 30, 93, 108, 135, 144
lilly pilly 12, 29, 46, 127
lily-of-the-valley 73, 93, 129, 144, 164
limes *see* citrus
liriopes 67
lobelias 205
loganberries 117
lomandras 33, 46
loquats 45, 65, 117, 126
lotus 219
lovage 108
lupins 140
lychees 117, 118, 218
lycoris 156, 200

magnolias 147, 154, 221
mandarins *see* citrus
mangel-wurzel 57
mangoes 19, 34, 45, 47, 69, 87, 117, 124, 125, 180, 196
mangosteens 87
manures 75, 121, 197, 199, 223
chicken 28, 47, 167, 174, 180, 181, 208, 218
cow 14, 60, 67, 75, 167, 221
horse 223
pig 75
sheep 46, 60, 67, 75, 78, 83, 108, 186, 199, 223
maples 73
marigolds 33, 49, 125, 205
marrows 209–10
mealy bugs 81, 137, 141
medlars 51, 117
melaleucas 71, 137, 216
melons 207–13
pests and diseases 63, 194
T 18, 34, 103, 123, 157, 180, 196, 217
M 21, 36, 160, 182, 198, 220
C 201, 222
Michaelmas daisies 140
michelias 221
midgen berries 48
mint 92
T 86, 103, 123, 141, 157, 181
M 88, 105, 126, 143, 160
C 128, 145, 162
mites 16, 21, 100, 112, 121, 124, 192
mitsuba 83
mizuna 83
mock orange 202
mondo grass 67, 156
mosquitoes 16, 219
moss 38, 69, 107
mountain laurels 202
mulberries 65, 106, 117, 202
mulch 12, 17, 64, 68, 146, 188–9
murrayas 30, 46
muscari 59
mustard 55, 57, 83, 94
T 86, 103, 123
M 21, 36, 49, 70, 88, 105, 126

mustard greens 83
myrtles 48

nandinas 127
nasturtiums 33, 205
native irises 103
native plants 22, 31, 33, 36, 66, 82, 84–5, 122, 144–5, 154, 195
  climbers 183
  fertilising 31, 129, 145, 223
  groundcovers 194
  new varieties 64, 162
  planting 146, 162, 203
  potting 195, 200
  pruning 22, 31, 71, 102, 145, 183
  see *also* specific plants, e.g. callistemons
nectarines 24, 70, 72, 106, 117, 129, 143, 185
nematodes 54
nemesias 85, 102, 146, 163
nerines 33, 144, 156, 179, 200, 203
netting
  excluding birds and bats 19, 104, 218
  excluding insects 81, 201
New Guinea winged bean 142
New South Wales Christmas bush 200
nigellas 163, 179
November lily 90, 144, 193
nut trees 128
  see *also* specific nuts, e.g. almonds

okra
  T 34, 86, 103, 123, 141, 180, 196, 217
  M 182, 198, 220
oleanders 135
olearias 12
olives 89
onions 23, 47, 51, 57, 70, 88, 91, 105, 108
  companion plants for 128
  M 126, 143, 160, 182, 198, 220
  C 128, 145, 162, 184
  see *also* ornamental onions; spring onions
oranges see citrus
orchids 98, 155
  see *also* specific orchids, e.g. cymbidiums
oregano 222
organic gardening 10
ornamental onions 202
outdoor furniture 215
oxalis 138

pak choy 83
palms 30, 34, 49, 142
pandoreas 183
panolas 85
pansies 33, 39, 49, 85, 91, 125
parrots 126
parsley 22, 49, 57
  T 123, 141, 157, 180, 196, 217
  M 70, 88, 105, 126, 143, 160, 182, 198, 220
  C 72, 91, 162, 184, 201, 222
parsnips 57, 124, 160
  T 124
  M 126
  C 23, 38, 51, 162, 184, 201, 222
passionfruit 66, 82, 104, 146, 158, 161, 199, 216
Patersonia (native iris) 103
pawpaws 47, 69, 87, 104, 118, 124, 141, 158, 196, 218
peach leaf curl 70, 104, 121, 139, 143
peaches 24, 70, 72, 97, 117, 129, 143, 185, 202
peanuts 18, 190–1
pear and cherry slugs 16–17, 49
pears 21, 49, 65, 84, 106, 109, 118, 118–19, 122
peas 55, 57, 88, 97, 163
  T 47, 67
  M 36, 49, 70, 88, 105, 126, 143, 160
  C 91, 128, 145, 184, 201, 222
  see *also* snow peas
pecans 128
pelargoniums 18, 33, 46, 90
pennisetums 46
peonies 74, 93, 129
perennials 52, 67, 90, 123, 139, 155
perilla 83
persimmons 65, 117, 118, 126
pesticides 10, 148–9
pests see specific pests, e.g. aphids
petunias 39, 179
philadelphus 154, 202
phlox 67, 140
phormium 156
photinias 46
pineapple lilies 156, 200
pineapples 103, 124, 196
pistachios 127, 128
plectranthus 46, 219
plumbagos 66
plums 24, 38, 65, 106, 118–19, 119, 122, 129
poinsettias 20, 102, 123
poisonous plants 135
poisons 135

pollination 86, 96–100, 117–19
by hand 22, 194, 209
pomegranates 117
ponds 14–16, 18, 109, 219
poppies 52, 91, 108, 146, 163, 205
portulacas 179
possums 180
potatoes 62, 63, 75–8, 86, 97, 124
no-dig 145
pests and diseases 63, 192
varieties 76–8
T 67, 86, 103, 123, 141
M 36, 70, 88, 143, 160, 182, 198, 199
C 23, 145, 162, 184, 201, 222
potted plants 37, 82, 87, 107, 186, 197, 203, 214, 215, 217, 221
powdery mildew 20, 39
in cucurbits 180–1, 194, 208–9, 216
in dahlias 184
in gerberas 22
in grapevines 121, 201
in hydrangeas 22
in pawpaws 124
in roses 20, 193
primulas 33, 52, 85, 108
prostantheras 183
proteas 65, 195, 203
pruning 32–3, 66–7, 102, 122–3, 139–40, 155–6, 178, 195, 216–17
after bushfire 12
after frosts 155
by dogs 134
fruit trees 19, 21, 24, 32, 37, 84, 110, 189
grapevines 21, 106, 124
hibiscus 140, 159
hydrangeas 66, 90, 105, 163
native plants 22, 31, 71, 102, 145, 183
roses 87, 107, 110, 111–16, 146, 193, 200
psyllids 29
pumpkins 51, 57, 72, 157, 185, 209–10
pollination 22, 97, 209
powdery mildew in 20, 180–1, 194, 208–9
varieties 210
T 18, 86, 103, 123, 141, 157, 180, 196
M 36, 182, 198, 220
C 184, 201, 222
pyrethrum 172

quinces 65, 106, 117

radicchio 162, 182, 184, 198, 201
radishes 57
T 18, 34, 123, 141, 157
M 21, 36, 70, 88, 105, 126, 143, 160
C 23, 38, 51, 72, 91, 108, 128, 145, 162, 201
rainbow chard 206
rambutans 196, 218
Rangoon creeper 183
ranunculus 52, 60, 62, 90, 93
raspberries 21, 23, 38, 70, 72, 92
regeneration after bushfire 12–13
reticulation 17, 64, 126–7, 177, 193, 215
rhizomes 62–3
rhododendrons 50, 109, 147, 171
rhubarb 23, 31, 38, 51, 72, 91, 92, 106, 163, 182, 199
rocket
T 47, 67, 86, 123, 141, 157
M 126, 143, 160, 182, 198
C 145, 162, 184, 201
rockmelons 22, 211
root-knot nematode 54
rootstock 82, 101, 178
rosella
T 18, 34, 157, 180, 196, 217
M 21, 36
C 201, 222
rosemary 18, 22, 144
roses 38, 39, 50, 65, 82, 87, 93, 123, 146, 178
climbing 195
cuttings 93, 203
fertilising 138, 200
heat-proofing 189
pests and diseases 20, 137, 193
pruning 107, 110, 111–16, 146, 193, 200
rudbeckias 67, 123, 140, 163
rust 48

saffron 62
saltbush 12
salvias 39, 46, 66, 179, 205
sandy soils 187
santolinas 12
sapodillas 45
sapotes 118
sawfly larvae 16
scabiosas 67
scaevolas 33, 194
scale 44, 81, 121, 137, 184
Scarborough lilies 140
sedums 140
seed collection and storage 85, 130, 220

seedlings 65, 85, 93, 199, 217, 218
shadecloth 19, 21, 110, 188, 198, 199, 215
shallots 23, 38, 51, 72
shasta daisies 67, 110
silver birch 73, 93
silverbeet 51, 57
  T 18, 34, 47, 67, 86, 103, 123, 141, 157
  M 21, 36, 49, 70, 88, 143, 160
  C 23, 38, 51, 72, 91, 162, 201, 222
slaters 160
snails and slugs 24, 29, 63, 81, 90, 100, 154
snake beans 143, 157, 180, 196, 217, 220
snake gourd 143, 160
snakes 159
snapdragons 49
snow peas 91, 108, 128, 162
snow-in-summer 12
snowdrops 52, 59
soil types
  acid/alkaline 120
  clay 91
  sandy 187
sollyas 183
Solomon's seals 144, 164
sooty mould 137–8
sparaxis 59, 90
spinosad 176, 177, 218
spring onions 185
  T 18, 47, 67, 86, 103, 123, 141, 157, 180, 196, 217
  M 21, 36, 49, 70, 88, 143, 160, 182, 198
  C 23, 72, 162, 184, 185, 201, 222
  see *also* onions
squash 57, 209–10
  pests and diseases 63, 208–9
  T 180
  M 182, 198, 220
  C 184, 201, 222
star fruit 87, 158
stenocarpus 11
stephanotis 135
stink bugs 37
stocks 49, 85, 108
stone fruit *see* specific fruits, e.g. apricots
strawberries 45, 65, 166–71, 182, 184, 194, 216
  pests and diseases 160, 167, 169
  varieties 169–71
  T 68, 86, 141
  M 22, 37, 70, 143, 160, 182, 198, 220
  C 184, 201
Success (caterpillar spray) 44, 95, 125
succulents 18, 121, 179
suckers 178, 193
sulphate of potash 24, 161
  for fruit 28, 87, 104, 124, 128, 141, 143, 161
  for indoor plants 183
  for irises 89
  for sweet peas 41
  for vegies 73, 79, 128, 161, 166
sunflowers 49, 146, 217
swedes 94
  T 47, 67, 86
  M 70, 88, 105, 182, 198
  C 23, 38, 51, 72, 145, 162, 184
sweet corn 23, 31, 47, 97, 157, 182, 220
  pests and diseases 104, 125
  T 18, 34, 47, 67, 86, 103, 123, 141, 157, 180, 196, 217–18
  M 21, 160, 182, 198, 220
  C 23, 184, 186, 201, 222
sweet peas 31, 40–2, 50, 87, 144, 146
sweet potato 62, 103, 104, 141, 181
  T 34, 67, 86, 103, 123, 141, 157, 180, 196, 217
  M 182, 198, 220
sword beans 217

tamarillo bushes 89, 219
tamarinds 69, 104
taro 18, 21, 34, 62, 141, 142, 157, 181
tatsoi 83
termites 157, 159
teucriums 46
themedas 46
thrips 124, 136–7, 184
thyme 86, 222
tip cuttings 18
tomato russet mites 192
tomatoes 38, 57, 72, 97, 157, 165–6, 166, 178, 215, 220
  pests and diseases 54, 125, 173, 192
  T 18, 34, 47, 67–8, 86, 103, 123, 141, 157, 180, 196, 217–18
  M 21, 143, 160, 182, 198, 220
  C 23, 72, 163, 184, 201, 222
transplanting 44–5, 64, 73, 82, 88, 103, 122, 127, 189, 199, 202
tree dahlias 67, 123, 142
trees 11–12, 195, 215, 216
tritonias 90

trumpet vine, orange 127
tuberoses 73, 108, 140, 202
tubers 62
tulips 50, 52, 59, 90, 196
turf see artificial turf; lawns
turmeric 48, 62, 68, 87, 142, 181
turnips 23, 38, 47, 51, 70, 72, 143, 145, 160, 162
two-spotted mites 16, 21

valottas 108
vegie patches 31, 44–5, 47, 57, 83–4, 205–6
  aesthetics 204–6
  crop rotation 49, 51, 54–7
  feeding and fertilising 65, 193–4, 205
  flowers in 49, 86, 156, 160, 205
  heat-proofing 188, 198, 215
  maintaining 91, 104, 145, 157
  in pots or bags 88
  preparing beds 47, 162, 194
  revamping 160
  seedlings 178, 185, 218
  siting of 206
  watering 220
  see also specific vegetables, e.g. zucchinis
Venus flytraps 63
verbenas 49, 205
viburnums 33, 46, 147, 154, 171, 202
violas 49, 108
violets 85

wallflowers 33, 52, 108
wandering jew 135
waratahs 144
wasps
  citrus gall 16, 106, 139
  parasitic 85, 148, 192
  as pollinators 98, 99
  predatory 44, 149, 154, 156
water chestnuts 62, 84
water features 18
  see also birdbaths; ponds
waterlilies 14–16, 161, 219
watermelons 18, 20, 22, 34, 194, 212–13
wattles 81, 85, 145, 202
waxflowers 85
webbing caterpillars 16, 137, 154
weeds 20, 36, 47, 64, 105, 107, 159, 195, 197, 204–5, 223
  see also specific weeds, e.g. bindii
weigelas 154
Western Australian Christmas tree 200
westringias 46, 202
wetting agent 17, 52, 71
white cedar moths 171–2
whitefly 63, 95, 192
wildflowers 50
wilting 189
windflowers 179
wisterias 22, 197
worm farms 30, 65

yams 68, 181
yarrows 67, 91, 123

zephyranthes 164
zinnias 179
zucchinis 57, 182, 199, 206, 207–9, 213, 220
  pests and diseases 63, 180–1, 194
  pollinating 22, 209
  T 18, 34, 141, 157, 180
  M 21, 36, 160, 182, 198, 220
  C 23, 184, 201, 222

Also available from Fremantle Press

'Sabrina's gardening knowledge combined with her wicked sense of humour and passion for the environment guarantees an amusing and practical answer to almost any question.'

—*Josh Byrne*

Also available from Fremantle Press

'Small in size, it's packed with practically all you need to solve citrus problems and grow the juiciest fruit.'
—*Better Homes and Gardens*

More non-fiction from Fremantle Press

Real Food for Dogs and Cats is for every pet lover who wants to ensure their cat or dog has the best chance of a long and healthy life.

This no-nonsense guide to natural and balanced pet nutrition has simple, practical and effective ways to keep pets in top condition.

More non-fiction from Fremantle Press

When push comes to shove, there is nothing as fundamental as a well-functioning bowel. This comprehensive guide is full of practical advice, helpful tips and clear explanations for how to obtain and maintain a successfully working bowel.